Amphibians As Pets

Books by the Zapplers

THE WORLD AFTER THE DINOSAURS by Georg and
Lisbeth Zappler
THE NATURAL HISTORY OF THE TAIL by Lisbeth Zappler
AMPHIBIANS AS PETS by Georg and Lisbeth Zappler

AMPHIBIANS AS PETS

GEORG and LISBETH ZAPPLER

with photographs and drawings by Richard Marshall

Doubleday & Company, Inc., Garden City, New York

ISBN: 0-385-04821-1 Trade
    0-385-08581-8 Prebound
Library of Congress Catalog Card Number 72-92252

The authors wish to thank the New York Zoological Society and Mr. Peter Brazaitis for their help in providing photographic specimens.

Contents

Amphibians As Pets

1. Meet the Amphibian

There are evenings in the spring when the earth seems entirely silent. Walking along the banks of a stream on such an evening, one can feel a great sense of loneliness. Somehow every living creature seems to have disappeared. Suddenly, in the midst of this frightening silence, a peculiar croak resounds. The silence returns, but is broken again and again by this same amusing, reassuring sound. One is not alone in an empty world. A small comrade is close by and is making his presence known. It is, of course, a frog.

It is a strange thought that at one time in the earth's long history, the only sound ever heard was the voice of an amphibian. This was because, other than a few scorpions and spiders, amphibians were the only animals alive on the land. In the surrounding waters, many forms of life flourished, but the early amphibians were the only animals with backbones on land.

Modern amphibians do not give the appearance of cour-

This amphibian has an enormous voice for so small a creature. The barking tree frog *(Hyla gratiosa)* is so-named for the quality of its call, when it is up in the trees. During the breeding season, this call changes and sounds more like rapidly repeated gunshots.

ageous travelers. But, of course, as with all life, appearances are deceptive and times change. Early amphibians bore little resemblance to those we know today.

The word "amphibious" means having a double life. It is quite descriptive of the class of animals bearing it. Frogs, toads, newts, salamanders, and the wormlike, tropical caecilians are modern members of the group. They are animals who are able to live on land as well as in water. Some remain in the water most of the time, while others are almost completely terrestrial. Caecilians actually live under the ground. Most amphibians employ both environments and are able to cope well with either. By and large, amphibians live a large part of their lives on land and return to the water mainly to reproduce. The young, therefore, are born in the water. For that reason, they are usually quite different in appearance from their parents. They are born equipped for aquatic life and must be transformed, as they mature, to be able to enjoy a terrestrial existence.

Amphibians are remarkably versatile animals. Although dependent upon water, they can be found in very dry areas. Even some deserts are inhabited by toads and frogs, who always manage to locate a small puddle to accommodate their needs. High mountain ridges are scaled and colonized by tiny salamanders. Deep jungles provide homes, not only on the ground, but, for some enterprising frogs, even in the trees. The only continent in which some species of amphibian cannot be found is Antarctica. No amphibian lives in salt water, so do not look for them in the oceans. Anywhere else, you may look forward to an encounter with a small double-living friend.

If you will stop to consider, for just a moment, the complexities of a life in which part of the time is spent on land and part in water, you will begin to appreciate the amphibian body. A fish is a lovely creature with its sleek torpedo shape and brilliant scales. But, removed from its watery environment, a fish could not survive for more than a few hours. The stumpy, popeyed frog, however, manages well anywhere. The reasons for this versatility can be found in the marvelous amphibian body.

No feathers, fur, or scales cover the body of an amphibian. Like people, amphibians have naked skins. Their bodies are pleasant to touch, for they feel smooth and cool. The amphibian's skin serves many purposes. It keeps the animal from drying out while on land and helps the lungs in their job of respiration. Also, nakedness increases sensitivity, as the nerve endings are close to the surface, and changes in the environment are thus quickly detected. The skin, therefore, is the most vital organ of touch possessed by amphibians.

Just beneath the skin are a number of glands. The mucous glands secrete the fluid that is responsible for keeping the animal moist while on land and also lubricates while the amphibian is immersed in water. Mucous glands are scattered over the entire body and, while very tiny in size, are capable of secreting an enormous quantity of sticky fluid when stimulated.

Tree frogs have glands in the toes that release a substance like glue. This enables the climber to cling to a vertical tree trunk or an overhanging branch.

Lungless salamanders rely on secretions of glands located in the groove between nose and lips to free the nostrils of water and mud.

Some male frogs have other kinds of glands that have developed from the mucous set. These are located in the chest and in the thumbs and are there for breeding purposes. Their sticky secretions make it possible for the male to hold onto his slippery mate while in the water. Male salamanders

The green tree frog (*Hyla cinerea*) is able to cling to the sides of his tank by virtue of the sticky secretion that flows from glands in the toe disks on his feet.

rely on secretions from glands on their chins to attract the female's attention.

There are also granular glands in the skin of amphibians which form the main means of protection for these small animals. They secrete a substance very irritating to the eyes and mouths of animals which might like to try a diet of frog legs. In some instances, this secretion is highly poisonous and can cause nausea and paralysis in small animals. Usually, when an amphibian is capable of producing such a devastating effect upon an enemy, it is brilliantly colored.

Even among all the warts on the marine toad's (*Bufo marinus*) body, the large swelling behind his eye is noticeable. This is the paratoid gland, from which a secretion of thick, white, poisonous fluid flows whenever he is attacked by enemies.

So the vivid red or yellow of some frogs forms a warning to stay away. But some amphibians, like the drab brown marine toad, are highly poisonous and do not advertise the fact.

Unlike our skin, that of the amphibian allows water to pass through in both directions. The rate of passage varies with the amount of moisture in the environment, the extent of dehydration in the animal, and the exact species involved. Toads have fairly dry skin which allows for little water loss, enabling them to live in drier areas than most frogs. Amphibians that live in the desert are particularly quick to absorb water during infrequent rainfalls.

Just as the smooth skin permits water to pass in and out of the body, it also allows for an exchange of gases. Oxygen is taken in and carbon dioxide passed out through the skin. The blood vessels are very close to the surface and able to absorb the necessary oxygen directly. Thus, the skin assists the lungs in breathing and, indeed, in some cases, as with the lungless salamander, takes over the breathing function completely. This is important to the amphibian while on land, for its lungs are not as efficient as ours and cannot handle all the oxygen the animal needs. Skin breathing is even more important when the animal hibernates underwater. During the cold months, many amphibians sink down to the muddy bottoms of lakes and ponds to sleep out the bad weather. There, with the body functions slowed down, less oxygen is needed and the amphibian is able to get all it needs through the skin without having to surface for lung breathing.

The outermost layer of skin is shed at frequent intervals throughout the year. You will be unlikely to find a frog or a salamander skin lying about as you would a snakeskin, however, for the amphibian includes this old skin in his diet. As the skin begins to peel, the amphibian begins to swallow and the swallowing motions help in loosening the skin still

19

further. After shedding, the amphibian looks shiny bright and new, but is soon covered again with the dust that serves as camouflage.

Very young amphibian larvae have only one layer of skin. Tiny hairlike structures grow from it and the motion of these hairs sets up currents in the water around the infant. These currents move the immature tadpole forward through the water to new sources of food, until the larva is old enough to move its body and tail with its muscles.

Caecilians, which are burrowing animals, have different needs and therefore different skins than do salamanders and frogs. The skin of a caecilian feels smooth, but beneath the top layers, tiny scales can be found imbedded.

Different ways of life demand different responses from the senses. Therefore, each group of amphibians have a unique type of development of vision, hearing, smell, taste, and touch — each of them meeting the needs of the owner.

Frogs and toads have their eyes set at opposite sides of their heads, looking out in different directions. When an object is close at hand, they are not able to focus upon it with both eyes. Therefore, these animals are usually rather farsighted. If they are the sort that live on flying insects such as butterflies and mosquitoes, this farsightedness is a decided advantage. They are able to spot their dinner at long range and judge exactly the right second at which to leap in order to intercept flight.

For a toad or frog interested in crawling things, like earthworms, somewhat nearer vision is needed. These hunters do not notice the wriggler until it is quite close. If it gets too close, however, the amphibian must back off a little way to see it properly before striking out at it.

This kind of eyesight is particularly beneficial in escaping from enemies. Frogs and toads, living on the ground, would make easy prey for larger meat-eaters if not for the fact that they can see forward, backward, sideways, and upward simultaneously.

Frogs and toads are very sensitive to differences in light. If you try to sneak up on one, you will find that, although his back may be turned, the moment your shadow falls across his body, he will be off in a bound. Those frogs and toads that feed by night are able to enlarge their pupils as do cats.

A thick fold of skin over the upper part of the eyeball forms the eyelid of toads and frogs. It is immovable as it has no muscles. Sometimes the bottom lid also lacks muscles. For this reason, some amphibians have developed an additional transparent fold of skin. This fold is called the nictitating membrane. It can be drawn over the eyes by muscles which surround the eyeball. Because of its transparency, even when the animal has drawn it up in sleep, he is able to view the outer world.

Toads and frogs have really beautiful eyes. The black pupil is usually horizontal, but sometimes is vertical as in cats, and, occasionally, it has a scalloped outline. The iris surrounding it is always a lovely color and is patterned by lines of gold or silver or red.

Salamanders have more pupil and less iris than their cousins, with less color in the iris. This is because they are primarily night hunters and need the enlarged pupil to receive the maximum amount of available light.

Most salamanders and newts have their eyes set closer together than do frogs and toads. But the hellbender, with its very wide head, has its eyes set so far apart that it can never focus both on a single object. However, as this animal feeds strictly by night, the senses of smell and touch are much more important than that of sight.

Some salamanders that live in dark caves are completely

Like most frogs and toads, the bullfrog (*Rana catesbeiana*) has extraordinarily beautiful eyes.

blind. However, in some species, where the young are born outside the cave, the larvae see well and do not lose their vision until they move into the cave at maturity. If forced to remain out in the open, they will go on seeing normally after maturing.

Many of the underground caecilians are blind, for their eye muscles and nerves have completely ceased functioning. Indeed, the bones of the skull frequently grow right over the eye sockets. For an animal living below ground, the sense of sight is unnecessary, and smell and touch play a much more important role in the business of living.

Just as it is necessary for a land-living animal to keep its skin from drying out, it must also have a way of keeping the eyes moist. To accomplish this, amphibians, like all terrestrial animals, have eye glands to lubricate the eyes. These glands and the eyelids, as well, are formed just before the larvae metamorphose. Some salamanders, therefore, that retain their larval state throughout life, never develop glands and lids at all. But, since their entire lives are spent in the water, such development is as unnecessary as it is for fishes.

You can tell which amphibians have the best hearing from the volume of sound produced by the animal. Frogs and toads, who communicate vocally, have a well-developed sense of hearing. In most frogs and toads, if you will look just behind the eye above the end of the mouth, you will see a round, shiny membrane of skin. This is the frog's "ear." It is actually the same mechanism — the eardrum — that is found in humans. There is one species of frog, however, living in Siam, which has an external opening with the eardrum well below the surface. But for most frogs and toads, the drum is clearly visible on the same plane as the side of the face. It is sometimes protected by a rim of thick cartilage, but more often it is flush with the skin. The distance at which a particular species of frog can hear sound depends on its life-style. Those species which communicate with others of their kind at a long distance hear better than those which "speak" only at close proximity. For instance, the male spadefoot toad, living in desert conditions, signals loudly after a rainfall to call the female to an available puddle to lay her eggs. It is necessary for her to hurry to the spot, from any distance whatever, to take advantage of the newly

The large round spot on the side of the green frog's *(Rana clamitans)* face is actually his eardrum.

created breeding ground quickly, for it may evaporate before long.

Most salamanders and newts make only small sounds. The Pacific giant salamander is an exception and can produce a loud barking noise as well as an earsplitting scream when in danger. However, most salamanders have to be content with little squeaks. As none of them has external eardrums, all "hearing" is done by the forelegs which are able to pick up ground vibrations.

Caecilians are completely voiceless. Probably they do not hear at all, but then there is little to hear if your home is a deep burrow.

Animals that live in caves or burrows are more dependent upon their sense of smell than they are upon vision. The same applies to those who live by night. Consequently, frogs and toads that are essentially diurnal (moving about in the daytime) see better and smell less than those who are nocturnal. Also, aquatic amphibians that feed in rapidly moving water are less likely to be able to find their food by sight than they are by smell.

The sense of smell in amphibians operates not only through cells in the nostrils, but also in a special area of cells in the nasal passage. This extra smelling device is called Jacobson's organ. It is found in snakes and lizards as well as in amphibians. Some aquatic salamanders lack Jacobson's organ, but the other salamanders and newts all possess it and in the frogs and caecilians it is very well developed. When the animal takes some food into its mouth, Jacobson's organ tests it for desirability. If unsatisfactory, the animal is able to spit out the food before it reaches the vulnerable stomach.

The nostrils are on the tip of the snout, sometimes on a raised surface (like a nose), but more often on a flat plane.

Even when an amphibian, such as the lungless salamander, needs no nose mechanism for breathing in air, it still has nostrils for smelling.

Caecilians have a very well-developed sense of smell and a marvelous mechanism for using it. In a little groove between the eye and the upper lip, lies a tentacle which can be brought forward and moved from side to side. The base of the tentacle is in contact with Jacobson's organ. When some item of food is encountered by the moving tentacle of the blind caecilian, tiny bits are quickly tested by the organ.

To the caecilian, the tentacle is an organ of touch as well as smell and its great sensitivity makes up for the animal's lack of vision.

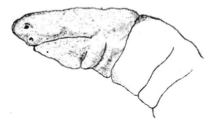

This odd head belongs to one of the wormlike caecilians (*Caecilia tentaculata*). In the small groove between the blind eye and the lips is a tentacle used for testing the desirability of food.

As in humans, the sense of taste is very closely allied to the sense of smell in amphibians. There are, however, separate mechanisms for the two senses. The taste buds are arranged in groups of cells found in the tongue, along the jaws, and in the palate of all amphibians.

When an amphibian is responding to a taste sensation, he swallows or snaps his jaws. When the sense of smell is stimulated, he will move his head or body.

Although insects and worms are quite unappetizing to us, amphibians have definite preferences in this range of diet and unappealing ones are spit out — proving that the sense of taste is well developed.

The lateral-line organs of some amphibians indicate very clearly these animals' intermediate position between fish and fully terrestrial vertebrates. These organs, possessed by fish but not by higher vertebrates, are to be found in aquatic salamanders, frog and toad larvae, and even in some adult frogs. Lateral lines are clusters of tiny cells that form in rows of pear-shaped pits on the head and body. They pick up vibrations in the water and localize the center of gravity, and so the body stays balanced.

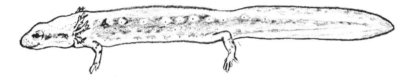

The small pits that appear down the sides of the body of this two-lined salamander (*Eurycea bislineata*) larva are lateral-line organs. In aquatic amphibians, they serve to help in maintaining balance in the water.

When an amphibian, such as the newt, becomes terrestrial for a while after an aquatic existence, the lateral-line organs disappear beneath a covering of skin. When back in the water, the organs reappear.

Amphibians have the means to conquer and digest some of the most plentiful protein available to the world. They fill their bellies regularly with worms and insects. This kind of high-protein diet provides energy for living processes, restores worn-out tissues of the body, and allows for growth. Any surplus food is transformed into carbohydrates and stored until needed. It can then be turned into sugar, which supplies the energy required by all living animals. The ability to store extra food enables the hibernating species to get through the winter in good shape. Amphibians never develop any great concentrations of fat, however, as do some birds and mammals. But their relatively slow metabolism burns up food at a slower rate and allows them to operate at maximum efficiency, even when they are very lean.

The feeding equipment of amphibians varies with the mode of life. The true toads are completely toothless. Frogs usually have teeth only in the upper jaw. These teeth are capable of gripping prey tightly, but they are never used for chewing and very rarely for biting. However, one species, the South American horned frog, is very fierce and uses his powerful jaws and sharp teeth as aggressively as a tiger.

In most frogs and toads, the teeth are well assisted by an amazing tongue. A few frogs, called aglossids, are tongue-less and use their hands to stuff food into their mouths. But, usually, the tongue is all important. Unlike our tongue, the frogs' and toads' is fastened at the front of the lower jaw, while the back is loose. When the mouth is closed, the tip of the tongue faces backward, toward the throat. When ready to strike at its prey, the frog opens his mouth wide and the tongue pops out in a forward position. Within the mouth are numerous glands that coat the tongue with a sticky secretion. Any unlucky insect that is struck by this quick, mobile tongue is then hopelessly stuck.

Once the prey is in the mouth, a muscular contraction takes place which forces the eyeballs down into the roof of the mouth and assists the tongue in pushing the insect down into the gullet. This contraction accounts for the blink which accompanies every swallow of the frog.

Some salamanders also have rather sticky tongues. Many have a fascinating mushroom-shaped tongue which they are capable of shooting out over an enormous distance. Some salamanders have teeth in the jaws, while others have only a few on the palate. In place of the jaw teeth, some have developed powerful horny plates, similar to the beak of a turtle. One almost legless salamander, *Amphiuma*, has very sharp teeth and bites viciously in self-defense.

As for the caecilians, they have two rows of teeth in the upper jaw and one or two (depending on the species) in the lower jaw. They have no trouble holding onto their prey.

Now, what becomes of the food once it leaves the mouth? As with most of us, it passes into the esophagus, which in the amphibians is a straight tube lined with small hairlike struc-

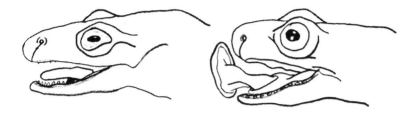

The salamander tongue is an important food-gathering instrument. The dusky salamander (*Desmognathus fuscus*), left, has the tongue attached in front and free at the sides and back. In the two-lined salamander (*Eurycea bislineata*), right, the mushroom-shaped tongue is supported on a central stem and is free all the way round.

tures called cilia. The food is coated with mucus in the esophagus and the cilia help the muscles in moving the slippery food through to the stomach.

Once within the stomach, special muscles move the food around and mix it with gastric juices. If, however, the food turns out to be disagreeable, frogs are able to turn their stomachs inside out and push them straight out through the mouth (like emptying a garbage pail). If the food is good, it is treated with chemicals, such as hydrochloric acid, and enzymes like pepsin, which begin the process of digestion. Some food may be held back at this point for storage. Since it is important to the amphibian to have extra food, the stomach of many can be expanded to a tremendous degree.

The intestine of amphibians starts as a tube of uniform width, then widens to form the large intestine. Most caecilians have the entire intestine straight. In the main, larval amphibians eat plants rather than insects and this kind of vegetarian existence demands a more involved intestine. Most tadpoles, then, have intestines that are looped and coiled into a long spiral tube. The few carnivorous tadpoles of the world have much shorter digestive systems.

Within the intestine are glands which secrete a substance carried by the blood to the pancreas. This stimulates the pancreas to begin the second stage of digestion through the release of the pancreatic juices. When the food reaches the pancreas, it is broken down and is well on the way to becoming the product necessary to the amphibian's health.

The final process of digestion is accomplished by the intestinal juices produced by mucous glands that line the walls of the intestines.

The products of digestion are absorbed by the walls of the intestine. From here, they are transported by the blood to those areas of the body needing building-up and replacement of tissues. Those not needed immediately are taken to the liver. Although the liver takes up a large area in the body of an amphibian, it does not actually contribute to digestion. Its function is to store some of the fat products formed from the protein food. Just before hibernation, the liver of some amphibians may double its size with stored food.

A few frogs also store some fat in their necks and under the skin in other parts of the body. Salamanders frequently store fat in their tails.

Indigestible food is held for a while in the large intestine as feces. Both the feces and the urine are excreted at intervals through a single opening called the cloaca. The cloaca is a sort of combined rectum and bladder, found not only in amphibians, but also in reptiles and birds.

All amphibians seem to be able to fast for very long periods without harmful effect. Certain salamanders have been known to exist for over a year without food. This remarkable ability surely accounts for their successful existence in frequently difficult environments.

Breathing or respiration is the way in which all of us supply our tissues with much-needed fuel. This fuel is a gas we call oxygen. Oxygen is passed into the tissues by way of the blood stream. Just as important as the taking in of oxygen is the elimination of another gas, carbon dioxide, which is unhealthy to our system. The blood stream picks up carbon dioxide from inside the body at the same time that it releases the oxygen required by all parts of the body. That way a continuous balance is maintained. Under conditions where not enough oxygen is available, carbon dioxide accumulates in the body and the cells become paralyzed and may die. This is true of all animals.

As we have already mentioned, an amphibian's way of breathing is different from ours. We use only our lungs to take in oxygen and get rid of carbon dioxide. Amphibians usually use lungs, too, but they also have skins that are moist and porous and that function as an additional site of gas exchange. Some amphibians, having no lungs at all, are extremely dependent on this kind of skin breathing.

Young amphibians, before metamorphosing, have gills for breathing. For the aquatic way of life to which they are restricted, this means of breathing is the most efficient. It enables the animal to draw oxygen from the surrounding water, rather than the air. The gills of young amphibians sprout from the sides of the neck and are sometimes quite ornate. As the tadpole matures, the gills are absorbed into the body. Lungs begin to form and the mature amphibian can then leave the water, able to breathe oxygen from the air. Some amphibians never metamorphose and spend their entire lives in water. Thus, the axolotl, for instance, retains its gills throughout life.

Whether lungs, gills, or skin are used by an amphibian for breathing, the mechanism is basically the same. The large arteries carrying the blood away from the heart break

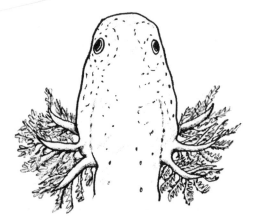

Most amphibians begin life with gills for breathing; then, as they mature, develop lungs. The greater siren (*Siren lacertina*), shown here, is aquatic all its life and retains its plumelike gills.

down into smaller vessels which in turn split up into many tiny capillaries with thin walls. These tiny capillaries then reform into small veins which then become large veins carrying blood to the heart. Because the walls of the capillaries are so thin, gas exchange is easy there. With gills, the gas exchange is carried on between the air in the water and the blood in the capillaries. In skin breathing, the exchange can take place in water or air. Lungs are paired elastic sacs within the chest lined with blood capillaries. A very large quantity of oxygen may be brought in and a proportionately large amount of carbon dioxide released through the lungs. But the method is effective only on land.

Even those amphibians possessing lungs do not breathe exactly as we do. We breathe with the help of muscular movements within the walls of our chest. Amphibians breathe by moving the floor of the mouth, pulling air into the mouth. Then they close their nostrils and force the oxygen into their lungs. You can see a sort of quiver in the throat of a frog as it pulls in air.

The bone structure underlying the skin and flesh of an amphibian varies in the different forms. Generally speaking,

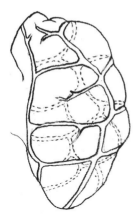 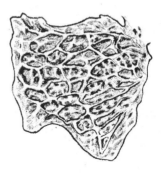

After the gills have been replaced by lungs, young amphibians are able to breathe oxygen from the air instead of from the water. They are then ready to begin their terrestrial existence. All lungs function in the same way, but may look somewhat different. Here is the lung of a tailed frog *(Ascaphus truei)*, left, and an opened lung of a marine toad *(Bufo marimis)*, right.

even in adult amphibians, the skeleton is partly made of cartilage or gristle with the rest consisting of solid bone. The small vertebrae that make up the spine may number only nine as in the frogs and toads, but can reach as many as 250 in salamanders and caecilians. Usually there is only a single vertebra that anchors the skull to the back. Thus amphibians are a practically neckless group and do not have the ability to turn their heads without moving the whole body. The salamanders, with dozens of vertebrae between the front and hind legs, are elongated aquatic forms that swim through the water like eels. The dwarf sirens and the amphiumas, the "congo eels," are good examples. More generally, however, salamanders have only some fifteen jointed vertebrae making up the back regions — with another twenty-five or so constituting the tail. The wormlike caecilians, who appear to be

33

all tail, have only a few tail vertebrae, but as many as two hundred vertebrae in the body proper. The tailless frogs and toads have a long bony rod rather than separate bony discs at the end of the backbone.

All vertebrates with legs have bony structures called limb girdles attached to the backbone. The pectoral or shoulder girdle carries the front legs and is attached to the column right behind the neck. The rear legs are anchored by way of the pelvic or hip girdle which is located near the vent or cloaca. The tail starts directly behind the hip girdle. Both limb girdles can be compared to V-shaped plates, closed on the underside, the open ends of each V attaching to the sides of the backbone. Each girdle is made up of separate elements fused together to form the kind of open ring just described. The shoulder girdle is attached by way of ligaments and muscles. The hip girdle is much more tightly affixed to the backbone by way of an actual bony fusion between a single vertebra, called the sacrum, and the uppermost elements of the girdle. The upper bones of all four legs are in turn socketed into round depressions on each side of the girdles. Thus, the limbs can support the weight of the body when the animal moves.

The legs themselves are made up of three main sections. There is the upper limb socketed to the girdles, followed by a lower portion which bears the hands and feet. In the hoppers, the frogs and toads, the hind legs are very powerful and the bony elements making up the spring mechanism are correspondingly large. The hind foot is tremendously lengthened and serves as a powerful lever against the ground when it pushes down, during the jump.

Salamanders have rather short limbs which they use not so much to lift themselves off the ground in the manner of a dog or horse, but more as jutting-out supports as they wriggle

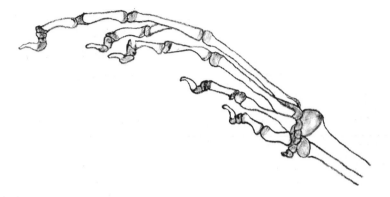

Skeletons tell stories to informed observers. This foot, with its claw-shaped toe bones, informs the expert that this frog is a climber, one of the members of the tree frog family, the little grass frog (*Hyla ocularis*).

from side to side. Salamander limb girdles are correspondingly small. The legless amphibians, the caecilians, have no hip girdle at all, and use a strictly snakelike method for getting around, above and below the ground.

The amphibian skull doesn't look at all like the solid, long box you may have in mind, if you are thinking of a human skull. It is made up mostly of cartilage rather than bone; also it is quite flat, looking a little bit like a filled-in horseshoe. There are large holes for the eyes, and the front edge constitutes the upper jaw. The U-shaped lower jaw is slung from either side of the hind end. The brain itself is so small that it takes up only a fraction of the total skull. It is located in a small cavity at the very rear. The legless amphibians have a more solid skull than either frogs or salamanders. In line with their burrowing existence, their skulls are ramming tools for driving the body through the soil.

If any group of animals is to be truly successful, an efficient method of reproducing its own kind is an absolute essential. For many amphibians, breeding is a complex matter, for although they may be terrestrial throughout their adult lives, they must return to the water to reproduce. Some have developed the ability to produce young on land in moist surroundings, but, for most, water is necessary. True, even a mud puddle is adequate for some, but others need large bodies of fresh water in which to mate and have young.

Because of the great diversity in methods of reproduction, there is no one time of year when breeding takes place. In desert-living types, for instance, any good rainfall is the signal for mating, whatever the season. Where young need a long time to mature, early spring mating occurs. Others, that develop quickly, can be produced later in the summer.

Mating can be a very elaborate ritual or a simple matter of fertilizing the eggs as quickly as possible.

Many amphibians lay eggs, but there are also those that retain their eggs within the body until the young emerge. Some species lay thousands of eggs at a time, while others have just a few. Some young look like small replicas of their parents. Many, however, bear scarcely any resemblance to the adults. In each case, there is a good reason for the differences involved.

The business of mating in all higher forms of life, involves two individuals, one male and one female, coming together to produce young. The female manufactures the eggs and the male fertilizes them. In any group of animals, this getting-together of the sexes is a serious business attended to at more or less regular intervals. Usually, there are clear-cut differences between the sexes — which are known as secondary sexual characteristics. These characteristics may be there permanently throughout adult life, or they may only appear at mating season.

Many times, size indicates sex. In amphibians, the adult

female is frequently larger than the adult male. Of course, this is not always so. The tiger salamander and the hairy frog, for instance, have males considerably larger than their females. Sometimes adults of both sexes are the same size.

Male frogs can sometimes be distinguished by dark patches on the throat. Male bullfrogs have noticeably larger eardrums than females.

All these characteristics are permanent. Of a more temporary nature is the peculiar glandular growths found on the male hairy toad. Every breeding season, long, slim, hair-like strands cover the sides and thighs of the males of this species. Later, this hair disappears.

Male European newts go through an elaborate metamorphosis during the breeding season. At other times of the year, they are terrestrial, but become completely aquatic in order to mate. The toes become webbed for swimming; the tail, too, adapts to water by becoming broad and enlarged. A lovely frilled crest appears on the back and tail. This crest is of a beautiful red color which highlights the already striking black-spotted brown body.

Usually males and females appear in equal number, but mating in amphibians is primarily a random matter. Permanent pairing-off rarely occurs.

Well, then, how do these animals meet at the appropriate times? Frogs and toads, we know, gather together at a large pool in enormous numbers every year, most frequently during the spring. It is the male who arrives at the chosen place first and from there utters his familiar croak. At breeding time, with many males croaking together, it can create quite a din. The purpose of all the noise is to lead the females to the mating grounds. Some male frogs and toads have large sacs beneath their chins which enable them to issue particularly loud calls. When relaxed, the sac appears as a loose flap of skin. But when in use, it is filled with air, forming a bubble that is sometimes so large that the male cannot see around it while in the act of calling. The first appearance of this pouch in a male frog is the indication of his new sexual maturity.

When the female frogs have answered the summons and appear on the scene, mating takes place. Each male hops from female to female without favoritism. In his enthusiasm, he might occasionally land on the back of another male, but, then, there would be a warning grunt, quite different from the mating call, to point out his mistake. A female who has already laid her eggs makes another kind of sound to ward off unwanted male attentions.

Sometimes, it is not the calling of the males that brings frogs together. The smell of certain water vegetation blooming in the spring lures the common frog to a certain pool. Frequently the sudden rush of spring water caused by increased oxygen will summon the frogs to their reproductive business.

The burrowing caecilians are the only amphibians that have internal organs for fertilizing eggs. This is a South American species, *Siphonops annulatus*.

For the voiceless newts and salamanders, mating is quite different. Males and females have to look longer and harder to find each other. When they do meet, it is up to the male to attract the female by means of his beautiful color or interesting odor.

Male and female caecilians must squiggle around underground to find each other. Males have special organs for internal fertilization of the females' eggs, so there is no danger of two members of the same sex becoming confused about each other.

Perhaps you are wondering how amphibians of different species manage to recognize the differences and remain apart at mating time. This important separation is usually provided for by the nature of courtship. Male salamanders, for instance, have involved courtship rituals to practice before the female in order to stimulate her properly. Only one routine is recognized and approved by the female, so the distinction remains clear-cut. Some North American salamanders stand in front of the female and emit glandular secretions from their cloaca, which they waft through the air to her by use of the tail. If the female is of the same species, she will follow closely behind him with her snout pressed close to his tail. No other species is likely to find his behavior pleasing.

Secondary sexual characteristics also work to indicate differences in species. No two species of frogs, for instance, sing the same song.

So we see how the right two animals get together for breeding. Now, how does the actual mating occur? Once again, it varies with the animal.

Most frogs and toads have no elaborate courtship ritual. There are a few exceptions. For instance, male and female poison frogs of Central America play an involved game of leapfrog before actual mating occurs. But mostly frogs waste no time courting. The male simply hops onto the back of the first available female as she swims by. He clasps her tightly with his forearms in an embrace called amplexus. On some of his fingers, a special rough structure assures his tight grasp on the female's body. Sometimes these warty surfaces also appear on the hind legs or the belly. The female then stretches her body and lays the eggs. At the same moment, the male releases his sperm in fluid form. The sperm enters the eggs, which are then usually dispersed by the hind legs of the male. Once all this is accomplished, the male hops off and swims away in search of the next waiting female.

Tailed frogs are so-called because of the long, tail-like organ of the male. This is actually not a tail at all, but a long extension from the cloaca. These frogs, because they live in rapidly flowing water, practice internal fertilization, with the male using his special cloaca to deposit his sperm directly into the female's cloaca.

Most salamanders have a more complex premating ritual, with great variations between species in courtship dances and display by the male. Only in a few species is the court-ship casual. Hellbenders, as an example, have very non-chalant mating patterns. Here, the female simply lays her eggs and later some male she has never seen drifts by to spray them with sperm.

Usually, however, the male salamander must go to some-what more trouble to receive a sign of approval from the female. When she does issue such a signal, he emits his sperm, wrapped up in a jellylike package called a sperma-tophore. The female may then press her cloaca over the package to take it into her body, or she may use her hind legs to ram it in. In some species, the male actually pushes

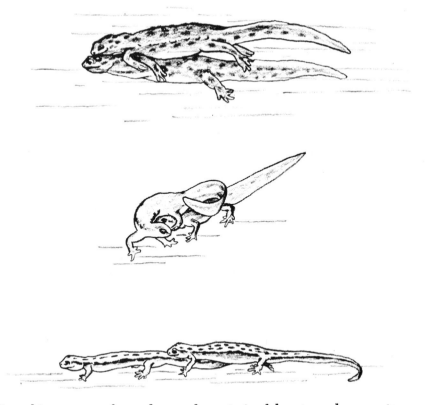

Courtship among salamanders and newts is elaborate and serves to keep the different species distinct. Illustrated here is the courtship of the waltl newt (*Pleurodeles waltl*) (top), the red-spotted newt (*Noto-phthalmus viridescens*) (middle), and the two-lined salamander (*Eurycea bislineata*) (bottom).

his spermatophore into the female's cloaca. In any case, once the spermatophore is in the female's body, the gelatin dissolves and the sperms are stored in a special sac called the spermatheca located in the roof of the cloaca. Later, as each egg is laid, the sperm is freed to fertilize it. Some species store the sperm for several months, so that the time of mating and the time of fertilization are quite distinct.

Male salamanders and newts fertilize eggs by means of a spermatophore, a kind of gelatinous packaging for the sperm. Here are spermatophores of a red-spotted newt *(Notophthalmus viridescens)* (left), a dusky salamander *(Desmognathus fuscus)* (middle), and a two-lined salamander (*Eurycea bislineata*) (right).

Very little is known about the subterranean caecilian's mating behavior. As the males have a sexual organ designed for putting in sperm, we can assume that fertilization is internal.

The kinds of eggs and the number laid by each amphibian female is once again highly variable, depending on species. One species of frog is known to lay only one egg at each breeding season, while some energetic female toads lay as many as 25,000 at one time. Some eggs are simply dropped in the water, while others are deposited in nests or watched carefully by a parent.

In general, those animals laying many eggs are less likely to make provisions for care than those with just a few offspring.

Amphibian eggs have a yolk surrounded by membranes, over which is a jellylike covering. They are usually laid in

42

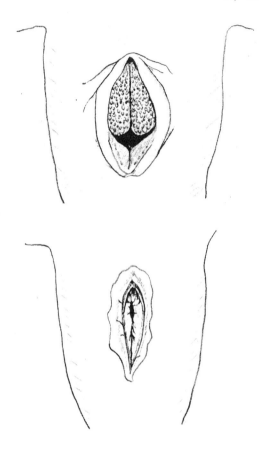

In amphibians, a single opening known as the cloaca is used for reproduction and excretion. Here is the cloaca of a male dusky salamander (*Desmognathus fuscus*) (top) and a female (below) of the same species. The small bumps are a clue to sex in most salamanders as they are usually found only in the male.

the water in clusters or strings of different lengths. But some species lay single eggs and attach them to stones or plants.

Those that lay eggs on land, and they are definitely in the minority, sometimes make small moist nests of pools in the holes of trees. There are tree frogs that build clay pools to house their eggs. A few amphibians even carry their eggs around on their bodies.

Parental care among amphibians is quite different from that shown by birds toward their eggs. Amphibians do not sit on their eggs in order for the heat of their body to help hatch the eggs. Their bodies are not warm enough to ac-

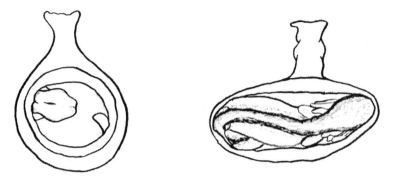

Within each small amphibian egg, a new life develops. Here, a red salamander (*Pseudotriton ruber*) embryo is shown as it looks while still in the egg.

complish this. Instead, they must depend upon the sun to do this job for them and, therefore, in the majority of cases the eggs are simply left exposed. The incubation period varies according to the temperature of the water or air surrounding the eggs. Some eggs hatch in just a day, while others take weeks.

The tiny amphibian inside the egg may develop glands on his snout which secrete a substance that dissolves the egg membrane near his head. This helps the young creature to escape from his egg. Other amphibians develop a small egg tooth on the upper jaw which is used to split the membrane.

The young salamander or caecilian that emerges from the egg usually looks very much like its parents, except for the fact that it has gills to enable it to breathe in water. Anyone who has seen a tadpole, however, knows that this is not the case with frogs and toads.

A tadpole appears to be just a large head attached to a tail. No legs or arms are in evidence. The large gills are

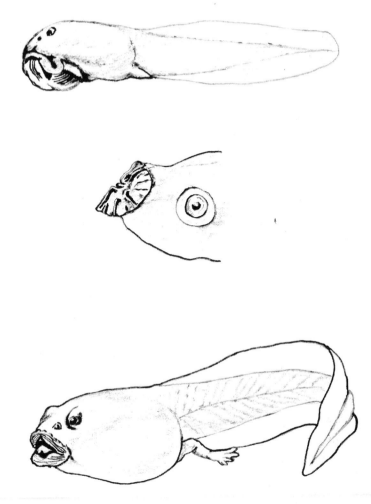

The diet determines the mouth shape of these tadpoles. At top is the larval form of a tailed frog (*Ascaphus truei*). The shape of its mouth is useful in scraping algae and small invertebrates from rocks at the bottom of the cold streams it frequents. The middle illustration shows the mouth of a narrow-mouthed toad (*Microhyla heymonsi*) tadpole. This animal gathers its food from the surface of a pond. At the bottom is a horned toad (*Ceratophrys dorsata*) larva with its broad mouth and strong jaws ideally suited for a cannibalistic existence.

obvious in the newly hatched larvae. But not all tadpoles look alike. Differences in living conditions produce different kinds of tadpoles. Those that swim in still water develop high crests on the tops of their tails to aid them in their free-swimming way of life. Others are more streamlined with a flattened body and low tail. Those living in damp air rather than water have even lower and longer tails. The structure of the mouth is also different in tadpoles with varying diets.

All newly hatched tadpoles are helpless little beings, barely able to wriggle over to some nearby water plant and cling for dear life. Each one feeds itself on what is left of its yolk sac. After a time, the external gills are covered over by a flap of skin and breathing is accomplished by internal gills. Gradually, the legs begin to appear; first the front ones, and then the hind legs. Once this happens, the tail begins to be absorbed into the body. With its disappearance, the tadpole has became a charming little frog or toad, just like its parents, except for its small size.

The young salamander's metamorphosis seems merely a matter of losing the external gills. (This, by the way, is the only change in developing caecilians.) But there are a few other changes in salamanders that are not so obvious. Young salamanders have no eyelids, while the adults do.

In most amphibians, before metamorphosis is complete, the lungs appear and take over the job of the gills. A new system of blood circulation develops. The legs become strong enough to carry the animal on land.

With all these changes, it is not so surprising to find that there is also a change in diet. Salamanders, who are similar to the parents in external appearance, are also meat-eaters at an early stage, but tadpoles usually start life as vegetarians and only become carnivorous as they mature.

Some amphibians do not go through any metamorphosis at

46

all. These are animals that are born on dry land and so hatch out of their eggs as miniature adults. Such is the case with the Alpine salamander and some lungless salamanders. Some of the narrow-mouthed toads as well as some frogs also boast fully mature offspring. In these land-born types, there is much more parental supervision of the eggs than is usual among amphibians.

There are also certain tree frogs that dam up the water in shallow areas close to the banks and make small mud-walled pools in which to lay eggs. In this protected environment, the young develop in relative safety from predators.

Some frogs make nests of foam. At the time of egg-laying, the female also extrudes a substance that looks like egg white which is beaten into a meringue by the father's hind legs until it floats at the top of the water. Here the young remain to grow and mature until the nest disintegrates. Sometimes, such foam nests are constructed on land and the foam is particularly important here, for it keeps the young from drying out.

There are foam nests made in leaves by tree frogs, but other sorts of leaf nests are also made. Here, it is the jellylike mass surrounding the egg that acts like a glue to hold the leaf rolled up.

Even the lowly caecilians practice a kind of child care. Frequently, female caecilians wrap themselves around their eggs as a way of ensuring sufficient moisture. Some salamanders also care for their eggs in this manner; many never stray from their eggs. Usually, it is the female salamander who acts as protector, but sometimes the male is the guardian. Indeed, some devoted fathers stand by constantly flicking their tails through the water, so that oxygen bubbles are formed around the eggs.

Frogs rarely stay near the eggs in this manner, but there

are some who carry their eggs around with them. Some South American tree frogs actually have a pouch on the back for the carrying of eggs. In some species, the male actually places the eggs in the female's pouch with his hind legs. Others are simply rolled down into position as they are laid.

The amphibians most famous for child care are the midwife toads of Europe. In this group it is the male who assumes the role of protector. Midwife toads do their pairing-off on land and, as the female lays her long string of eggs, the male wraps it around his hind legs. There they remain entwined for the three or four weeks it takes to incubate them. The female goes merrily off on her way immediately after laying the eggs, leaving her patient mate to care for their twenty to sixty offspring. The male withdraws to his hole, now spending all his daylight hours there, only venturing forth in the evening to search for food and moisten the eggs attached to his legs. At the right moment, he goes for a dip in the nearest pool, leaving the eggs to hatch and develop in normal tadpole fashion.

Other male amphibians showing great parental care are the tiny, one-inch-long Darwin's frogs, who store their young in their enormously enlarged vocal sacs. To judge from the size of the pouch, one would think there would be a huge voice issuing forth from this small amphibian. But the voice is weak. The whole purpose of this structure is incubation. The way it works is that a group of male frogs surround the twenty or so eggs recently laid on the ground and fertilized. They guard that clutch for as long as three weeks. Then, when the embryos within begin to move around, each male flips out his tongue and picks up several eggs, sliding them back into the pouch. There the young remain throughout the larval stage, emerging as perfectly formed little froglets of about a half inch in size.

The small arrow-poison frogs of South America also act like devoted fathers. Here, the eggs are attached to the back of the male where the young remain after hatching in numbers of about twenty or so. As they grow larger and form a bulkier load, the male is forced to look for bigger and bigger holes in which to hide. They do not leave the father's protection until they are quite mature, at which time he immerses himself in water and allows them to swim free.

Some amphibian mothers achieve protection of their young by keeping them within their bodies as do human beings. Some caecilians remain within the mother's uterus, feeding from nutritive material that is somehow secreted in this area. Fire salamanders live within their mother's body for ten months, emerging in the water as almost completely metamorphosed amphibians. They have well-formed arms and legs, but there are still gills present to assist them in the watery life they lead until, as fully mature adults, they take to the land. Alpine salamanders have about fifty eggs reaching the oviduct of the mother, but only one or two actually form embryos. The yolk of all the others are used as food by those developing.

The length of time it takes for a young amphibian to develop into a fully mature specimen varies tremendously according to species. Some are quite adult in less than a year; others, like the bullfrog, take four or five years to develop completely. Some amphibians grow in size without making the change from aquatic to terrestrial form. This process, known as neoteny, can be seen in some salamanders which reach adulthood without losing their gills or other larval characteristics. Although they look like overgrown babies, they are capable of mating and having young. This kind of growth usually occurs in species living their entire lives in cold, deep water.

The life span of an amphibian is also variable. Some species must live out their whole existence in a year, while others have a much longer period on earth. The record for longevity seems to be held by the giant salamander of Japan, which has been known to reach the ripe old age of fifty-five years.

2. Ancient Amphibians

When we begin to think about animals as a whole group, certain questions begin to form in our minds. It is important to know how they developed and where they stand in relation to other groups — in short, what is their place in nature?

With each group in order to learn the complete story, it is necessary to go far back in time to see just how they evolved. This evolutionary picture is particularly interesting with the amphibians, for they are unique in their position as half-land, half-aquatic animals.

Although their own history is very long, there were many events that had to occur before the amphibians could make an appearance on earth. At the beginning, all life was aquatic. Although much land was available, no one had yet inhabited it. The first animal life appeared in the form of small water-living invertebrates (animals without backbones). After much time, with many changes having occurred, animals with rods similar to spinal columns inside the body began to live in the seas. Such animals, resembling the young stages of living sea squirts and the transparent arrow-shaped animals called lancelets, finally gave rise to fishes — the first animals with backbones.

It is possible for an animal to live on land without a backbone or vertebral column, if they remain fairly small. Indeed, one form of life, the scorpions and spiders, made it to land a little while before vertebrate animals. But, to successfully colonize the solid ground with its strong gravitational pull, a sturdy spine is necessary for any animal with any bulk. So the development of the vertebral column was a most important occurrence to our own as well as the amphibians' history.

Early fish appeared in many forms along the evolutionary path which led eventually to all the modern fishes. One natural "experiment" resulted in fish with lungs rather than gills. The development of lungs allowed the fish to breathe air as well as water, an important feature to those living in shallow areas which occasionally dried up. In addition to the lungs, paired fins, developed on either side of the fish's body, were also put to good use on land, for they could serve as limbs with which to propel the body forward from one pool to another. Many other changes had to occur before these fish became amphibians. Some of them will be quite apparent to you if you will note carefully the transition that occurs in your pet amphibian as it goes through its metamorphosis from aquatic larval form to mature terrestrial form.

There are many problems connected with life on land, unencountered in a life in the waters. These were the problems that had to be faced and solved by the first terrestrial vertebrates — the amphibians.

The most serious obstacle to overcome was the difference in breathing. Obtaining oxygen from the water is quite a different process from obtaining it from air. Those early fishes that evolved lungs as a solution to the business of moving from puddle to puddle as each dried out, made the first contribution to the eventual conquest of land. Watching the gills of a tadpole gradually becoming the lungs of a frog is like watching millions of years of evolution in miniature.

The lunged fishes had gills in addition to lungs, because most of their breathing was done in the water. The lungs were used only on those occasions when the fish were forced by drought or foul water conditions to breathe in air. The early amphibians had to develop lungs strong enough to reverse the emphasis so that most breathing could be performed on land.

A second problem to be solved was that of drying-out. An adaptation to permit the animal to hold onto the body fluids while away from water had to come about. This meant that the lovely, shiny fish scales, so useful for streamlining purposes in water, had to be abandoned as they were not an adequate body covering for terrestrial life. A tough skin, enclosing the flesh and preventing evaporation of the body fluids, was the eventual solution to this problem.

Now it was time to cope with the pull of gravity. Going onto land means struggling with an extremely powerful tug from beneath and, to contend with this, a strong spinal column and legs had to evolve. A sturdy interlocking structure of discs in a horizontal column down the back, complete with all the necessary muscles, eventually adapted the amphibians for terrestrial life. At the front of the column was located a strong supporting shoulder girdle. At the back, the hip girdle developed. The girdles in turn articulated with the limbs.

The limbs were important not only in supporting the body in its fight against gravity, but also as a means of moving from place to place. For an aquatic animal like a fish, the muscular side-to-side movement of the body, which is possible only because of the flexible internal backbone, is a highly efficient method of transportation. But, on land, one foot in front of another is a better method. Therefore, the paired fins of a fish were transformed into limbs.

Look closely at an aquarium fish. You will notice two sets of fins on either side of the body — one in the shoulder area and another farther back. You will see, as the fish swims, that these are used for balance. You will also see that they are the obvious means to eventual travel on land, by reason of placement on the body. On the other hand, the tail, so important to actual movement in water where it assumes the action of a propeller, is more useful on land as a balancing organ — something quickly observed in the nearest salamander as it moves.

Noting all the requirements for life on land, it is not surprising to discover that even the earliest amphibians — called ichthyostegids — were quite different from their forebears, the fishes. They must have had lungs that were much better developed than those of their fish ancestors and it was only in the larval stage that they would use gills as a main method of breathing.

Probably the first amphibians did have fish scales, but the thickened skin was to evolve soon afterward.

The backbone of even these first amphibian ancestors was much more complex than the simple discs of the lungfish. These were interlocking structures with strong muscular attachments. The swishing fish tail had already become modified into a shorter, less flexible structure and the paired fins had become stumpy little legs.

Although the progress made from lungfish to ichthyostegid was considerable, many other changes had to take place before the appearance of fully evolved amphibians. From the ichthyostegids, new lines of amphibians developed.

In time animals appeared with better breathing apparatus than that of their ancestors. The ichthyostegids had nostrils placed far down on the skull and the internal nasal openings were separated from them by only a thin piece of bone. Later amphibians had nostrils farther up on the face with passages to the inside.

These new amphibians had also developed even more complex, interlocking spinal columns, making them better able to endure gravity's pull. Because of this, amphibians were able to attain greater size. The limbs, too, became more modified for land living. All four legs had strong heavy bones, arranged in the same basic manner as our own. Hands and feet had five fingers or toes apiece and were connected by wristbones and anklebones.

The skull of the early amphibians was very heavy and very different from that of modern forms. It was solidly roofed by bone with just five openings: two for the nostrils, two for the eyes, and one between the paired eyes that worked as a sort of light receiver. There was a notch on either side of the skull for the eardrum and this characteristic was brand new with the amphibians.

There were teeth on the edges of the jaws and others in the front part of the palate. The enamel covering these teeth had folds in it resembling a maze or labyrinth and these amphibians are referred to as labyrinthodonts.

The labyrinthodonts evolved and developed in many directions. As successful amphibians, they began to appear in many different forms. Some were small and almost completely aquatic; others were large and terrestrial. *Eryops,* a five-foot meat-eater, competed well with the early reptiles which were just beginning to evolve.

Millions of years ago, this five-foot amphibian (named *Eryops*) lived along the banks of muddy rivers.

The reptiles, which had descended from other labyrinthodonts, became even better adapted for land living than their amphibian cousins and were later destined to take over dominance of the land. But at the time of *Eryops,* this amphibian was king of the world. It lived a lazy, crocodilelike existence, whiling away many hours in the muddy rivers. Bony nodules in the skin formed a protective armor against enemies. *Eryops* dined primarily on fish, but was able to catch many land animals as well.

After a while all the labyrinthodonts died out, but some of their descendants went on eventually to become frogs and toads. Of course, many changes had to occur first. The bones of the skull became smaller and there were fewer of them. The hip girdle became longer. Much later, the long tail was lost.

Now frogs and toads are characterized by an open, flat skull, much different from their ancestors' heavy, solid heads. The front legs are much shorter, while the hind legs are longer than those of the labyrinthodonts. The anklebones are particularly long and there is an extra joint there to give the leg more jumping power. The bones of the shoulder and the short front legs have been strengthened to take up the shock of landing.

All these great changes occurred long ago. Frogs and toads, in very much the same shape as today's species, have been around for more than 200 million years.

While all this was happening to the labyrinthodonts, another group of amphibians was developing in its own way — the lepospondyls. Lepospondyls were always rather small animals. They did not compete with their larger labyrinthodont relatives, but contented themselves with other habitats and food supplies. They lived in undergrowth near riverbanks or deep in the muddy swamps.

Many kinds of lepospondyls evolved. One group had long, snaky bodies; another had flat, broad bodies and heads. Some of the flat-headed amphibians became grotesque-looking creatures with wedge-shaped heads that resembled arrowheads.

Before dying out, the early lepospondyls left behind two lines of amphibians destined to live on to modern times as the salamanders and the caecilians.

3. Some Common Amphibians

Having reviewed the history of amphibians and examined the group as a whole, let us concentrate on some of those most frequently encountered in their natural habitats.

The Leopard Frog
(*Rana pipiens*)

The leopard frog is one of the most beautiful of all frogs. It is also the one commonly found all over North America. There are several races found in different geographical areas. Each race has its own characteristic coloring and marking. Generally speaking, however, a leopard frog is an iridescent bronze, with an underlying base color of olive-green. Soft yellow "leopard" spots dot the back and head. The belly is ivory toned. The skin is quite smooth except for two folds that run down either side from the eye to the hips.

The beautiful leopard frog (*Rana pipiens*) is easily found throughout North America in any area well populated by grasshoppers.

The more formal name for the leopard frog is *Rana pipiens*. *Rana* is the scientific name of the genus to which it belongs; *pipiens* denotes the species. The name of the family to which *Rana pipiens* belongs is the Ranidae.

The family Ranidae includes all those creatures known as "true" frogs. Other well-known members are carpenter frogs, pickerel frogs, and bullfrogs. There are representatives living on every continent.

The genus *Rana* probably originated in Africa and from there spread throughout the world. Most frogs of the genus *Rana* are slim-bodied, long-legged amphibians, with pointed toes; those of the rear feet are webbed. "True" frogs do not burrow, nor do they emit evil smells from their glands. Their only defense lies in escape. Therefore, they are built for speed. Leopard frogs are the best jumpers of the whole group, attaining distances of five feet or more in a single leap. They are alert to danger and will disappear quickly at your approach. All the Ranidae are diurnal (except during the mating season), as the insects they prey upon are day-living creatures. They have thin skins, so evaporation is something of a problem. Therefore, the "true" frogs live at the edges of ponds and streams and are frequently found floating in the shallow water.

The leopard frogs are more frequently encountered than other members of the family, for not only are they more common, but they travel greater distances from the water. You are likely to find them in meadows and orchards in the country, where they go to find the grasshoppers they so often eat.

Leopard frogs sleep away the winters in the muddy bottoms of their ponds, but they arise early. Only the spring peepers appear before them. You can hear their hoarse croakings in the evenings in strong contrast to the shrill song of the peepers. They have begun the chorus that announces that the time for mating has arrived.

If you are quiet as you approach the breeding grounds, you will be able to observe the males as they sit in the shallow water with only their heads protruding. Long vocal pouches extend from the front of the jaw to the shoulders. At the beginning of their song, a deep breath of air is taken. You will see the pouch over the shoulder begin to swell. As the swelling grows larger, the volume increases and the croaks are repeated four or five times. At the end of the song, the pouch very suddenly collapses, leaving only a wrinkled, baggy flap of skin to mark its position.

61

This frog has four distinct sex calls: the song that brings the female to the pond; a warning call given when one male accidentally grabs another; a sound the male makes when he approaches a female; and the female's rejecting grunt if she is not ready or has already laid her eggs.

As the female enters the water, a nearby male will circle her while singing his approach song. If she does not reject him, he will jump on her back and clasp her around her shoulders. She carries him around on her back this way for a while until both are ready to assume the right position for egg-laying. For the female, this means spreading the thighs and putting the heels together. The male raises his knees and puts his feet on her thighs. Now the female begins to pump out the eggs, as the male, bringing his cloaca next to hers, fertilizes them with his sperm at the moment the eggs appear in the space between their legs.

The eggs, laid in masses of from four to five hundred, may be attached to sticks and reeds, or may simply float free on the water. Each mass measures only about one or two inches across when first laid, but soon the jelly surrounding the eggs swells until it is almost five inches thick.

If you will search in the marshes among the cattails in shallow ponds right after you have heard the mating chorus, you are almost certain to spot some eggs. Why not take this opportunity for some close observation? The first thing you will notice is that each egg is very tiny, measuring less than 1/10 inch in diameter. It is a rich black color. The eggs, crammed close together, make the mass appear dark, although there is a transparent coating of gelatin surrounding each egg. The lower third of the egg on the underside of the mass is light. The dark part indicates the area where the actual tadpole will form; the white part holds the yolk upon which the developing embryo feeds.

If you continue to watch your frog eggs for a few days, you will note some fascinating developments. The egg will begin to swell. It also gets uniformly dark. Get yourself a magnifying glass and you will see a groove dividing the egg into two equal halves. Soon there will be a second groove at right angles to the first, making four equal parts. Now a horizontal groove appears, just above the center of the eggs and soon so many grooves run up and down and around each egg that there are too many parts to count. These parts are actually cells. In just this way is all animal life, including our own, begun.

Other things are happening to the now many-celled egg. After about twenty-four hours you should see a dark crescent-shaped line just below the middle of the egg. Another twelve hours and the crescent will become a circle. A small mass of yolk, forming a sort of plug, protrudes through this circle. This is the beginning of the digestive tract. The plug actually marks the point at the rear end of the frog.

By the third day, the developing eggs have changed from round to oval in shape and a long groove can be seen along the top. Now it is possible to tell which is top and bottom, front and rear.

You will no longer be able to see the yolk plug on the fourth day and the groove now runs the length of the egg. Two large folds, one on each side, are beginning to cover it. The groove and the folds will later become a tube. This tube is the beginning of the nervous system, with the brain at one end and the rest becoming spinal cord.

From now on, there is a radical change in the embryo each time you look at it. It gets longer and longer. The nerve tube is completely closed in. The tail projection shows clearly. The lumps in the front end indicate the position of the face, the suckers, and the gills. The body can be seen and is grow-

63

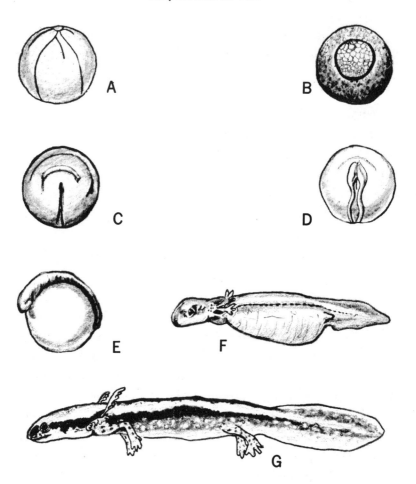

The development of an amphibian. A) About one day after laying, the egg (seen from the side) shows several grooves. B) After ten days, the egg looks quite different, with many cells apparent. The large circle marks the position of the future intestinal tract. C) At fourteen days the fold that marks the foundation of the nerves can be seen when observed from the top. D) The top of the egg at eighteen days. E) The embryo at twenty-two days. F) At seven weeks. G) Three months old. The larva is now easily recognized as a small mud puppy. (*Necturus maculosus*).

ing slimmer each day. The tail gets larger and you can see its fin. Soon the tadpole within the jelly begins to move and you can see the jerking that goes on inside.

After nine days, one big jerk will free each tadpole from its jelly casing. The new little life is exhausted after its escape and lies quietly for a while on the jelly. After a rest, it will wriggle through the water until it encounters a clump of weeds. With the two suckers beneath its mouth, the young tadpole will cling to its support for several days until it is sufficiently mature to move on.

At this point, the tadpole is quite strange-looking. It is only about 1/3 inch long with fingerlike gills extending from the sides of its neck. There are no eyes as yet, although there are small lumpy places on the head, where the eyes will be, and you can see these with a magnifying glass. With your glass you can also get a good look at the mouth and the suckers below it. These suckers work by means of a sticky secretion and not really by suction. The whole body is covered by tiny hairs called cilia which move back and forth, circulating the water around the tadpole. This helps the young creature to breathe until its gills are ready to take over the job. Once they are, the number of cilia are reduced.

After a while the head seems larger, because there are folds at the sides. These will keep growing until finally they have covered the gills, leaving only a slit. Then, the tadpole will use the gills as internal rather than external breathing organs.

The tadpole grows bigger and bigger, with the long tail providing most of the increased size. Finally, sixteen days after the eggs were laid, the tadpole is able to swim about in an active search for food. It will chew on water weeds or scrape algae from stones. Throughout its youth it has vegetarian habits. The tadpole does not retain its solid dull black color, but soon sports a number of golden dots on its body.

Life for the tadpole is fraught with danger. Many creatures make a diet of tadpoles and it will be lucky if it can escape all of them. Insect larvae, fish, turtles, and water birds will all be out hunting.

If the tadpole is able to avoid all his enemies, he will begin to metamorphose in about one month. Although the tail has grown until it reaches a length of about twice the size of the body, the hind legs are beginning to show. The front legs appear next. The head takes on a froglike appearance with appropriate eyes and mouth. Then, finally, the tail becomes absorbed.

Throughout the summer months, the spring breeding grounds of the leopard frogs abound with tiny froglets. They live in the shallow water among the weeds and wander about the nearby ground in search of their new food. Along with all the other transformations, a change of diet has also occurred. The froglets have become carnivorous and now live primarily on small insects. Young grasshoppers are a favorite food and spiders, beetles, and crickets are also eaten.

The young leopard frogs have long noses and slender bodies. The coloring is not quite the same as that of their parents. Sometimes they lack the characteristic spots and are instead a beautiful, shimmering metallic bronze or green all over.

Soon the young frogs will join the adults, feeding with them until the autumn frost sets in. Then, all will go together to the streams to sink down into hibernation. At the bottom, hidden away in the mud, they sleep, awaiting the early spring return to life and the calls to come and breed.

The leopard frog is the amphibian most often found in laboratories. Thousands of them are used every year for dissection and experimentation. It is also the frog served up on restaurant platters when you order frogs' legs. Many leopard frogs are also used by fishermen for bait. All these uses do not seriously deplete the frog population, and they make the leopard frog particularly valuable to mankind.

The American Toad
(*Bufo americanus*)

American toads belong to the family known as "true toads," the Bufonidae. The Bufonidae, like the Ranidae or "true frogs," has several genera in the warmer parts of the world, but one main genus, *Bufo*, found on every continent except Australia.

Unlike their cousins, the frogs, the true toads have fat bodies and short legs and are not very speedy travelers. To escape their enemies, they must rely on other characteristics. They blend in wonderfully with their surroundings; the brown warty skin looks just like the earth they sit upon. Whenever anyone approaches, they flatten out their bodies and lie perfectly still, so ·they are often unnoticed. If they should be seen, they roll over onto their backs and play dead. With all motion stopped (even breathing is suspended for a few moments), many enemies are fooled.

If this fails, the toad may burrow his way to safety. He is well equipped to do this, for there is hard skin on the hind feet and usually a sharp, horny spur used for digging. He can hollow out a hole very rapidly, backing in all the way until the earth falls in around him and affords him complete cover.

If, after all this, he is ferreted out anyway, he still has another protective method. All the so-called "warts" on a toad's body are really glands. The two largest ones, located behind the eyes, are known as the parotoid glands. From these comes a poisonous secretion which is irritating to mucous mem-

67

The American toad (*Bufo americanus*) is frequently encountered in gardens, where, because of his insect-hunting prowess, he makes a welcome guest.

branes. Any animal taking a toad into its mouth is likely to regret it. Human beings who have handled a toad must be careful to keep their hands away from their eyes and mouth until they have washed. There is no possibility, however, of getting warts from handling these amphibians.

Toads can live farther away from the water than frogs, for their skin is thicker and less susceptible to evaporation. For this reason, toads are more familiar than frogs to people living in the country, for they frequently inhabit our gardens. The toad you are most likely to meet in the eastern United States is the American toad.

American toads are squat animals with big heads. The females, who are larger than the males, can attain a length of 4½ inches. Their color varies from light to dark brown. Most, however, are a sort of reddish-brown with a few spots and blotches of lighter browns. The warts are frequently red or orange. Sometimes there is a light stripe right down the middle of the back. Unlike most animals, the female is much brighter in color than the male and her throat is a grayish-white while his is black.

On the head, over and behind the eyes, are kidney-shaped crests or ridges that are made by the bones of the head. There are four fingers on the hand and five webbed toes on the feet.

The toad's whole body is covered with many conspicuous warts, which some people find repulsive. The eyes of a toad, however, are breath-takingly beautiful and have even inspired poetry. The pupil is a shiny black, while the iris is golden.

If you go out in the spring to collect amphibian eggs, you will notice another way in which the toads differ from the true frogs. Rather than the shapeless egg mass laid by Ranidae females, American toads lay eggs in long tubes of jelly, with the tiny black eggs lined up neatly in a single row. Each female produces from four to twelve thousand eggs each year. The jelly tubes are clear and transparent when first laid but soon become twisted and muddy from the debris at the bottom of the pond. The eggs take from five to twelve days to hatch, depending on the temperature.

The transformation from tadpole to adult is very similar

to that of the leopard frogs. By mid-June thousands of tiny but perfect toads fill the ponds. Young toads go on land soon after transformation, as they cannot breathe in water once their lungs have fully developed. As they swarm up on the shores, they encounter their enemies. Snakes, hawks, owls, and ducks are all lying in wait and many thousands of the little creatures will be devoured.

The young toads that manage to survive their first summer burrow into the earth in the fields where they have been feeding. There, they sleep until the warm spring air rouses them. During the winter months they have grown to considerable size and have exchanged smooth skin for a tough, warty exterior. They are not yet ready for breeding, however. Sexual maturity is not reached until the age of three or four years. This is in keeping with the toad's longevity, for they are known to live to be more than thirty years of age.

Toads grow very rapidly. But their skin does not grow with them as ours does. When the old skin gets tight, the toad must shed it. (This skin shedding is typical of all amphibians.) During the summer months, when food is plentiful, the toad sheds about every three days. The process of shedding is smooth and quick, taking only about five minutes. The toad hunches up his back and bends his head down. The old skin splits right down the middle, from head to back, down the belly and across the chest from arm to arm. The toad pulls the loosened skin into his mouth. He will then eat it, and it has great food value. The skin is removed from the back end forward with the head skin being the last to go. The new skin is shiny and pretty, but within a few moments, it will be covered with earth, making the toad as well camouflaged as ever.

Toads act like homebodies. When a young toad is finally

70

When an amphibian grows, the top skin must be shed. Beneath it is a shiny new skin of the right size.

ready to mate, he will return to the pond in which he was hatched. The feeding place he has established while he was immature will remain his headquarters throughout his life. Any cool, moist place is a good home base. The toad lives in cellars, under porches, and in woodpiles. He comes out in the evenings to feed.

Any gardener must consider himself lucky if he has a toad policing his property, for the toad consumes many of those insects harmful to plants. With his limber, front-hinged tongue, he grabs locusts, beetles, lice, and caterpillars by the thousands.

Having stuffed himself with insects throughout the sum-

71

mer, the toad sleeps away the winter. Using his sharp spurs, he backshuffles his way into a deep burrow, snuggles in, and leaves the cold world above. When he awakes, if he is fully mature, he will be stirred to join others of his kind returning to the breeding pond. Once there, he will fill his vocal sac and begin to sing. The song of the toad is one of the prettiest in nature. It is a sweet trill that seems to come from many directions at once. The call sounds appealing to us — to the female toads, who do not sing themselves, it is irresistible. They swarm to the pond and there begin the mating process — the start of a new life cycle.

The Common Tree Frog
(*Hyla versicolor*)

Tree frogs of the genus *Hyla* include some of the prettiest little frogs in the world. The family Hylidae is centered in tropical America. There are five genera now located in the United States. Species of the genus have spread to every other continent. Most members of the tree frog family have suction discs on the tips of their toes, with which they cling to any available surface. Their legs are usually long and thin, with thighs heavier than shanks.

Most frogs of the genus *Hyla* are tiny, usually under two inches long. In addition to the common tree frog, some of the better-known species are the spring peepers, the green tree frogs, and the squirrel tree frogs.

As you might guess from the scientific name of the common tree frog, its color is changeable. It might be white, gray, green, or brown. If it is in one of its lighter phases, you should be able to see a small star across the top of its shoulders and bands of darker color on its legs. When the overall color is dark, these markings blend in and are not visible. The belly is white. In the folds of the hind legs there are splotches of bright orange. Two white spots are on the face, one beneath each eye. Because its skin is rough and warty, the common tree frog is sometimes called a tree toad. For a tree frog, it is big; sometimes attaining a length of 2½ inches. The broad discs at the end of the fingers and toes secrete a substance that helps them to hang on anywhere. Common tree frogs can be seen, if you look closely, anywhere in the eastern half of the United States.

Common tree frogs come to the ponds to breed in the late spring. The male's call is a loud, birdlike trill that begins early in the afternoon and continues until long after dark. Tree frogs attach their eggs, either singly or in small groups, to the stems of water plants. These eggs are a light gray color on top and white below. They hatch very quickly, in just two or three days.

The tadpoles are not dark as in most other frogs, but bright yellow. They have orange eyes and a beautiful red tail. Within a very short time, about three weeks, the tadpoles are well developed and even have the hind legs beginning to show. Less than two months after hatching, the tadpoles have completely metamorphosed and are ready to leave the water. Although only about ½ inch long, they are ready to feed upon spiders, flies, and plant lice.

This small amphibian is usually found up in the crotch of a limb, where, because of its camouflaging colors, it can hardly be distinguished from the bark. On the tree can be found an extraordinary variety of foods. Flies, beetles, ants, and crickets are all likely to be in easy reach.

When hunting, the tree frog shows its great acrobatic skill. He has fine vision and can spot a small insect at a distance of more than two feet. He will take a long, flying leap at

73

anything. He simply spreads his arms and legs straight out from his body and glides. On the way back, the fingers and toes are spread, for all he needs is a single toe hold to keep him secure. The disc cuts down the atmospheric pressure exerting suction, and the sticky secretion works like glue. The moist surface of his belly and legs will also help to hold him firm on any leaf or window.

Common tree frogs sing all through the summer months, particularly at times of dampness. For this reason, they are called rain frogs and are considered to be weather prophets, singing their loudest just before a storm.

Red-spotted Newt
(*Notophthalmus viridescens*)

The red-spotted newt, so common in the eastern United States, belongs to a family with almost all its members in the Old World. The family Salamandridae has only two genera in this country, one in the East and one in the West. The western newts (genus *Taricha*) are larger than the eastern species and not so colorful.

Eastern newts of the genus *Notophthalmus* are mostly aquatic except for a transitional stage of about two years when they are terrestrial. In some areas, however, this terrestrial stage is omitted and the newts are permanently aquatic.

The red-spotted newt can reach a size of five inches in length, but is usually from three to four inches long. As an adult, it has an olive-colored back and a yellow belly covered with fine black dots. Along each side is a straight row of scarlet dots circled with black. The tail is flattened for efficient swimming.

Red-spotted newts are fascinating to watch as they mature,

74

for they go through many radical transformations. As larvae, they not only have gills as do the frogs and toads, but also balancers placed midway between their eyes and their gills. They are born with the front legs already "budded" and they have broad, fishlike tails.

The mature larvae have wedge-shaped bodies that are quite slim. Although both sets of legs are well developed, there are still gills, which now lie flattened along the back. There are small white dashes from the gills to the tail which indicate the presence of lateral-line organs.

By autumn, complete transformation has taken place. The gills are gone, as are the tail fins. We now see a recognizable newt. The color at this point is a sort of yellowish-brown and the characteristic spots on the sides are pink.

The next stage is unique. The young newt does not immediately assume the appearance and life pattern of its parents. In most areas of its range, there is an adolescent phase which is quite different. At this point, the newt becomes terrestrial. In a few localities where ground cover is not adequate or if there is a shortage of food on land, the adult state is reached immediately and the small amphibian remains aquatic.

But, if conditions are right, the spotted newt becomes a red eft. The skin becomes rough and thick. The overall color is a bright brick red with the side spots prominent. The tail is rounded. Red efts wander far from their pond and can be found deep in the moist woods where they feed on insects, spiders, and worms. For a year or so, the young newts continue to live in this manner. Then they make their way back to the pond. On the way there, or very shortly thereafter, they assume typical adult dress and begin their mature aquatic life.

The breeding season, which may extend from spring

through autumn, demonstrates another interesting difference in appearance. For the male is quite unlike the female. He develops a broad fin on his tail and his cloaca is swollen and protrudes. Black horny growths appear on his inner thighs and on the tips of his toes. His hind legs are much stouter than his front legs.

Newts have a much more elaborate courtship than frogs and toads. The male begins by clasping the female under her throat with his hind legs. He then bends his body into an S and rubs his head against hers. At the same time, he brushes her with his constantly swaying tail. Sometimes he shakes her rather roughly. After hours of this ritual, the pair separates. The male then begins to deposit spermatophores on the bottom of the pond. These are white and vase-shaped. The bottom portion is gelatinous with a stiff, spinelike structure rising from it. At the top is the round portion which contains the sperm. Each time the male moves on to deposit another one, the female comes along behind him. She presses her cloaca over the newly placed spermatophore and the tiny sperm cells then travel upward into her body to fertilize her eggs. She appears to take in only as many spermatophores as are necessary for the eggs she has within her, since quite a few of the male's offerings are ignored.

Male newts develop special secondary sexual characteristics during the breeding season. Here is a Japanese newt (*Cynops pyrrhogaster*) with his swollen glands, long fingers, and fancy tail.

The female lays her eggs one at a time and fastens them to leaves and stems of aquatic plants, away from swift currents. She holds the stem between her hind legs and pulls her thighs together, thus forcing out the eggs one at a time. Each egg is in a tiny envelope of jelly which sticks to the surface of the plant. A female can lay three hundred eggs at a time. The egg is brown at one end and light green at the other. Temperature is the deciding factor in hatching time. In warm weather, the larva may hatch in three weeks, but if it is cold, it may take five weeks.

Although adult newts breed only in the warmer part of the year, they are able to tolerate the cold very well and can ·sometimes be seen swimming in a pond beneath the ice-covered surface. If it is too cold, they will burrow into the mud at the bottom.

As adults, newts eat a large variety of meats. Worms, insects, and small frogs are all acceptable food. They themselves are relatively free from predators, for they are protected by a nasty-tasting skin secretion.

Dusky Salamander
(Desmognathus fuscus)

We have just discussed the newts; amphibians that spend most of their lives in the water, yet are dependent upon lungs for breathing. Dusky salamanders, like the rest of their family, the Plethodontidae, live practically all their lives on land and are lungless. Adults have no gills, either, but take in oxygen through their skins and the lining of mouth and throat.

The Plethodontidae is the largest family of salamanders in the world. One hundred and fifty live in the New World

77

and there is one other in Europe. They are all small to medium in size, the tiniest measuring a little over one inch and the biggest about eight inches. Such well-known forms as the spring salamander, the red-backed salamander, and the red salamander are all members of this group.

Dusky salamanders are the most common salamanders in the eastern part of the United States. Although there are many of them living near brooks and streams, they are not easy to see. They hide in crevices and under stones throughout the day and only come out after dark. Sometimes on rainy days, they do venture forth, but even if you should see one then, you would be unlikely to catch it. It is very alert and scurries away swiftly. If you succeed in grasping one, you probably won't be able to hold onto it, for it twists very vigorously and will even bite if necessary.

The dusky is aptly named, for it is rather drab in color. The adults are brownish-black above and gray below. There is an irregular row of black spots down each side of the back and a white line from eye to jaw. The larvae are brown with two rows of light spots.

The adults are rather stoutly built with hind legs longer and heavier than the forelegs. The tongue is attached at the front of the mouth and is loose at the back and sides. Although the lower jaw is hinged and attached in the same way as that of other salamanders, it is unable to move very much. The jaw is held rigid when the dusky eats and the upper jaw does all the work. This makes the entire top of the head move with each bite of food. The lower jaw is handy as a wedge when the salamander wants to dig in under a stone.

Most amphibians share a desire to be in contact with the sides of any hiding place they occupy. This habit is known as thigmotaxis. It is especially developed in the duskies, which have been found wedged into discarded glass bottles, peacefully sleeping (with heads turned toward the mouth of the bottle) in broad sunlight on the surface of the ground.

Courtship between duskies is more romantic-looking than in other amphibians. Because the male has a gland on his chin which secretes a substance irresistible to the female, he rubs noses with her. This "kiss" stimulates the female to follow behind him, picking up the spermatophores he has just deposited.

Most amphibians like this toad (*Bufo marinus*) lie with their bodies against the sides of their hiding places.

Fifteen or twenty cream-colored eggs, laid in two small grapelike clusters, are the result of this mating. The female retires to a small nest under leaves or stones. This nest is large enough to include mother as well as eggs, for, unlike most amphibians, duskies stay with their eggs. The mother lies with her body twisted so that it is in contact with all her eggs.

The female dusky salamander (*Desmognathus fuscus*) is one of the few amphibians that stays with the eggs until they hatch.

Each egg is only about ⅛ inch in diameter, but has three protective envelopes of gelatin, bringing the total size to about ¹³⁄₁₆ inch. In about eight weeks, the eggs hatch, the larvae measuring about ⅝ inch long.

The larvae, very surprisingly for amphibians, are not quite ready for aquatic life when born. Although they have gills, they remain on land, sometimes for as long as fifteen days, before finally entering the water. Once there, they will remain aquatic for about nine months, making the transformation to adult form in the spring. With the coming of the warmer weather, the duskies head for land once again, there to breed and spend the remainder of their lives.

Dusky salamanders congregate in large groups and can be seen piled on top of each other in dark, damp nests dur-

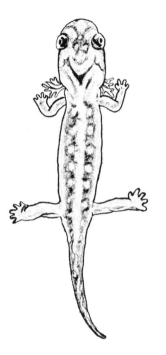

At hatching, the dusky salamander (*Desmoguathus fuscus*) larva is a highly appealing creature of about ½″ in length.

ing the hot daylight hours. At night, they come out to hunt, looking for the worms, slugs, and insects they particularly relish. In turn, they are hunted out by snakes and frogs.

The Mud Puppy
(*Necturus maculosus*)

Mud puppies, sometimes called water dogs, belong to a very small family, the Proteidae, which includes only two genera. One, *Proteus*, lives only in southern Europe, while *Necturus* is found in ponds and lakes in Canada and the eastern half of the United States. The animals of this family never metamorphose, but remain in larval form throughout their lives. Although they grow larger (some reach a length

81

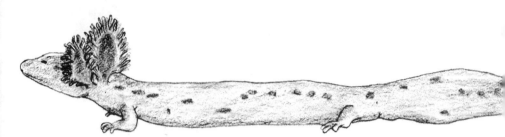

The mud puppy *(Necturus maculosus)* grows to be larger than most other amphibians, but retains its larval form throughout life.

of nineteen inches) and are able to mate, they retain all their infant characteristics. There are large gills and open gill slits. No eyelids develop. They do have front and hind legs, although these are not too obvious at first glance. Each foot has just four toes, a characteristic which sets them apart from other aquatic salamanders.

The most common of the two species of *Necturus* is the mud puppy, *N. maculosus*. Mud puppies are flat-bodied salamanders with big, round heads. The gills at the sides of the neck look like floppy ears. It is easy to see why they were given their common name, for they do look like small dogs scurrying along the muddy pond bottoms. Perhaps it was their appearance that gave rise to the myth that these salamanders bark. They do not. Like most salamanders, they have very small voices, scarcely more than a squeak.

The mud puppy has a soft brown color speckled with a few black spots on its sides and back. The body is streamlined and the tail is wide for more efficient swimming, as these amphibians never leave the water. They are difficult to observe in their natural habitat, for they are active mostly at night and spend the days hiding under rocks or debris. The color works as camouflage in the stream bottoms when the mud puppy does move around in search of food.

If the water in which a mud puppy lives is stagnant, you will stand a better chance of catching sight of it. For then the gills are expanded in an effort to gain more oxygen. The gills become bright red then, and wave back and forth through the water. In clear, cool water, the gills remain dark and are held close against the head. Mud puppies are fortunate in having lungs as well as gills and are also able to practice skin breathing. In this way, should some injury befall the spectacular gills, the animal can go on breathing.

From their hidden positions in the water, mud puppies are able to obtain a large variety of edibles. They dine upon snails, crayfish, insect larvae, small fishes, and the eggs of frogs and fish. In some areas, they eat so many fish eggs that the fishermen consider them to be a nuisance.

Autumn is the season for mating among mud puppies, although the female does not lay her eggs until the spring. Courtship continues for some time, with the male swimming over and under the female until she willingly picks up his spermatophores. These the female retains within her body until she lays her eggs. Occasionally a pair of mud puppies will remain together for some time after mating takes place.

When the female lays her eggs, she attaches them singly to the underpart of a stone or log. Each is a small, light yellow circle about ¼ inch in diameter. If the water is warm, they may hatch in about five weeks; otherwise nine weeks will be necessary. During that time, the female stays within the nest cavity. This is probably not due to any great maternal protective instinct, however, as many of her eggs are frequently eaten during this period by creatures smaller than herself without causing her any great concern. Most likely, it is the secluded spot itself which draws her, rather than her potential offspring.

The young, when first hatched, are only about one inch

long. Their front legs and fingers are well developed, but the hind legs point backward and have no toes yet. There is a broad, dark stripe down the middle of the back that runs from snout to tail. There is also a narrow yellow stripe on each side, from the gills back. In time the young mud puppy darkens to look like its parents, and grows steadily larger. By the time it is five years old, it has reached a length of eight inches and is ready for mating. The customary development of eyelids, however, and loss of gills never takes place. Jacobson's organ, used for testing objects in the mouth for edibility, is completely lacking.

Nevertheless, the mud puppy is tough and can be found active in all seasons. Even the coldest winter day will find a mud puppy walking slowly along the bottom under a film of ice. Although usually lazy in its movements, a mud puppy is capable of a good deal of speedy swimming if alarmed. The legs, then, are held close to the sides, while the broad tail does the job of propelling the animal rapidly through the water.

If the mud puppy's great success is due in part to its toughness, it is also partly due to its caution. If a mud puppy encounters a new form of food, for instance, it will swim for all it is worth in the opposite direction; the desire for safety overcoming its enormous appetite.

These are some of the most common amphibians found in the United States. Here are some others.

NAME	DESCRIPTION	RANGE	HABITS
GREATER SIREN (*Siren lacertina*)	Generally eel-shaped with feathery gills at the sides of the neck. No hind legs and front	Still waters from Washington, D.C. to Florida and Alabama.	Permanently larval. Completely aquatic. This is a nocturnal animal which feeds on

Name	Description	Range	Habits
	legs are small. Up to thirty-six inches in length. The smooth skin may be gray or olive.		worms, snails, and shrimp.
HELLBENDER *(Crypto-branchus alleganiensis)*	Olive with dark patches. Broad, flat body hides short, bowed legs. Loose-fitting skin. Huge, high-domed fore-head. Perma-nently larval. Eighteen inches long.	Western New York, Cen-tral Pennsyl-vania to Louisiana and west to Iowa.	Completely aquatic. Nocturnal. Feeds on any small water animal.
TIGER SALAMANDER *(Ambystoma tigrinum)*	Heavily built, black body, covered with yellow blotches and gray stripes. Seven to eight inches long.	Entire United States. Rare in East, more common in West and Southwest.	Adults live under stones and debris near ponds. Larvae found in cold, fresh water. East-ern species metamor-phoses norm-ally, but western types some-time remain permanently larval.

NAME	DESCRIPTION	RANGE	HABITS
SPOTTED SALAMANDER *(Ambystoma maculatum)*	Large, stout body with broad, flat head. Shiny black with yellow spots. Six inches long. Larvae greenish-brown with balancers and bushy gills.	Common in eastern and central United States.	Can be found under logs and stones in damp pastures or woodlands. Nocturnal. Larvae found in cool, fresh water.

The spotted salamander (*Ambystoma maculatum*).

NAME	DESCRIPTION	RANGE	HABITS
MARBLED SALAMANDER (*Ambystoma opacum*)	Gray with grayish-white bars. Five inches long.	Massachusetts to Florida, west to Oklahoma and Texas.	Found under stones on dry ground or burrowed under in sandy spots. Eggs laid on land. Hatch in rainy part of spring and autumn.

The marbled salamander (*Ambystoma opacum*).

Name	Description	Range	Habits
JEFFERSON'S SALAMANDER (*Ambystoma jeffersonianum*)	Brown. Sometimes has small, blue flecks on sides. Six inches long.	Vermont to Kentucky and west to Illinois.	Found under logs and stones and in rotting wood. Larvae live in marshes, ponds, and woodland streams.
LONG-TAILED SALAMANDER (*Ambystoma macrodactylum*)	Black with yellow strip down back. Two to three inches.	Common throughout Northwest from Montana to California and north to Alaska.	Damp, heavily wooded areas near cold streams and lakes. Also in semiarid brush and grasslands. Breeds before ice melts.
CALIFORNIA NEWT (*Taricha torosa*)	Brown, unspotted rough skin with yellow belly. Breeding male has large tail fin.	Coastal range of California from Mendocino County to San Diego County.	Transforms from aquatic larva to terrestrial adolescent like eastern newt. After return to water, an adult, however, may go back to land in times of drought. Can be found in ponds and

Name	Description	Range	Habits
			streams in aquatic stage. Under rocks and logs in terrestial form.
ARBOREAL SALAMANDER *(Aneides lugubris)*	Light tan or dark brown back with light spots on sides, legs, and tail. Cream-colored belly. Smooth skin. Well-developed legs. Tongue attached in front.	California.	Climbs trees up to 60 feet high. Lives in large groups in tree cavities, under rocks, in cellars and in mouse holes. Will bite in self-defense.
SLENDER SALAMANDER *(Batracho-seps attenu-atus)*	Slim head and body. Tail twice length of body. Short legs. Wormlike in appearance. Dark brown to black. Adults have broad strip of red or yellow down back. Five inches.	Oregon to Southern California.	Lives in rotted wood or bark. Curls up like snake with head in middle of coil. Wriggles rather than walks. Gregarious. Lays eggs in October after rains. Young hatch in spring.

NAME	DESCRIPTION	RANGE	HABITS
TWO-LINED SALAMANDER (*Eurycea bislineata*)	Small and slender with brown to yellowish body. Dark line down each side of back. Yellow belly. Three to four inches.	Maine to Florida and west to Louisiana.	Hides under flat stones in mud near brooks. Very quick and agile when aroused. Diurnal. Feeds on water insects, crustaceans, and worms.
PURPLE SALAMANDER (*Gyrinophilus porphyriticus*)	Pink to red with light line from eye to nostril. Stoutly-built. Eight and a half inches.	Maine to Ohio and south to Georgia and Mississippi.	Found in cold mountain brooks and damp forests. Nocturnal. Mate in autumn. Eggs laid from spring to following autumn. Young remain in larval stage three years.
MOUNT LYELL SALAMANDER (*Hydromantes platycephalus*)	Dark, mottled coloration. Short legs and tail. Webbed toes on hind feet. Mushroom-	California.	Lives under rocks at high altitudes. Mainly terrestrial. Nocturnal. Feeds on spiders,

90

NAME	DESCRIPTION	RANGE	HABITS
	shaped tongue is free around edges. Four inches.		termites, and beetles. Remains underground half the year to avoid the snow. Webbed feet act as suction cups in rock climbing. Tail turns down to form brake when animal goes downhill and swings from side to side as balancer when animal climbs.
RED-BACKED SALAMANDER *(Plethodon cinereus)*	Small and slender. Gray bars along back and tail. Five inches.	Common from Maine to Minnesota and south to Georgia and Oklahoma.	Completely terrestrial. Found in debris, such as rotting logs. Female guards eggs. Young born fully metamorphosed; remain with mother for a while.

Name	Description	Range	Habits
WESTERN RED-BACKED SALAMANDER *(Plethodon vehiculum)*	Stripe on back may be yellow, tan, or red. Four inches.	Oregon, Washington, and Canada.	Nocturnal. Sleeps in damp places, under logs and rocks. Lays eggs on land. No aquatic larval stage.
SLIMY SALAMANDER *(Plethodon glutinosus)*	Shiny black with silver dots along sides. Seven inches.	New Hampshire to Florida and west to Oklahoma and Texas.	Found in forest debris and in ravines. Completely terrestrial. Skin secretions are like glue.
RED SALAMANDER *(Pseudotriton ruber)*	Coral with black spots. Larvae brown. Four to five inches.	Common east of the Mississippi except in New England.	Found most frequently in and near small streams. Nocturnal. Lays eggs in fall. Larvae active in spring.

NAME	DESCRIPTION	RANGE	HABITS
PACIFIC GIANT SALAMANDER (*Dicamptodon ensatus*)	Large with massive head. Marbled with black spots on brown or gray base color. Twelve inches.	California north to Canada; also in Idaho and Montana.	Damp forests and rocky shores of lakes; usually under debris. Sometimes climbs trees and bushes. Eggs laid on land. Makes rattling sound when bothered.
TAILED FROG (*Ascaphus truei*)	Small and rough-skinned with light or dark brown back. Belly ranges from pink to dark gray. Pale yellow triangle on snout. Dark line from eye back. Flat, toadlike body. Two inches.	From Canada to Washington and Oregon and into northwestern California.; also in Idaho and Montana.	Lives in clear, cold mountain streams. Stays close to water. This is one of the few voiceless frogs. The "tail" is not a tail, but actually an external copulatory organ, only in male. This is the only frog to practice internal fertilization.

93

NAME	DESCRIPTION	RANGE	HABITS
PLAINS SPADE-FOOT *(Scaphiopus bombifrons)*	Looks like toad without parotoid glands. Spade is broad, black projection on inside of hind foot. There is a raised bump behind eyes. Dusky with yellow or red warts. Two and a half inches.	Great Plains from Missouri to Montana and Arizona and from Canada south to Mexico.	Loud quacking heralds breeding from May to August after rains. Eggs laid in shallow ponds. Adult lives in plains, hills, and river bottoms on prairie. Uses spade for burrowing; prefers sandy areas for easy digging.
EASTERN SPADEFOOT *(Scaphiopus holbrookii)*	Much like Plains Spadefoot, but with sickle-shaped spade and no bump between eyes. Two yellow lines down dark and two and a half inches.	Common in eastern United States, Gulf States, Texas, and north to Arkansas.	Stays in burrow until April; around ponds until August. Back to burrow after egg-laying. Voice is loud, unpleasant caw. Nocturnal.
CARPENTER FROG *(Rana virgatipes)*	Dark with four yellow stripes down back. Belly	Swamps and bogs from New Jersey to Georgia.	Voice sounds like hammer blows. Mating from

94

Some Common Amphibians

NAME	DESCRIPTION	RANGE	HABITS
	yellow with spots. No skin folds. Dark and light bands on thighs. Two and a half inches.		April to August.
BULLFROG *(Rana catesbeiana)*	Largest U.S. frog. Green above with dark markings; belly mottled. No folds in skin. Eight inches.	Found naturally throughout United States east of Rockies. Has been introduced west of Rockies and is flourishing in various western locales.	Can be found in ponds where it feeds on snails, insect larvae, worms, tadpoles, and other frogs. Hibernates longer than other frogs. Call like that of a bull not heard until June.

The bullfrog (*Rana catesbeiana*).

NAME	DESCRIPTION	RANGE	HABITS
GREEN FROG *(Rana clamitans)*	Head and shoulders bright green; body generally olive. Skin fold on each side of back. Five inches.	Common throughout eastern and central United States.	Found in small streams in swampy areas. Mates in May. Voice is low croak. Nocturnal. Almost entirely aquatic. Sometimes remains out of hibernation all winter.
WOOD FROG *(Rana sylvatica)*	Light to dark brown above; pure	From Atlantic Ocean to Mississippi	Wanders through woods, far

Some Common Amphibians

Name	Description	Range	Habits
RED-LEGGED FROG *(Rana aurora)*	Dark brown back with gray or brown blotches. Underside of hind legs bright red. Red mottling along sides. Five inches.	From Canada to Southern California.	Lives in marshes, streams, lakes, and ponds. Most commonly found in woods, but is sometimes in grass-lands. Voice is low cluck.
PICKEREL FROG *(Rana palustris)*	Much like leopard frog, but browner with more regular rectangular spots, not outlined in white. Belly white in front and orange behind and on legs. Three inches.	From Atlantic Ocean to Great Plains.	Usually found near cool streams and marshy ponds; but also frequents meadows. Feeds on flies, cater-pillars, and butterflies. Voice is like a loud snore. Skin secretes a substance distasteful to most pre-dators and poison-ous to other frogs.

97

NAME	DESCRIPTION	RANGE	HABITS
EASTERN NARROW-MOUTHED TOAD *(Gastrophryne carolinensis)*	Brown back has triangle of dark color surrounded by light stripes. Plump and short-legged with smooth skin. Head is small and pointed. One and a half inch.	From Maryland south to Florida and west to Texas and Oklahoma.	Because of burrowing habits, not easy to find, except while mating. Then, sheeplike bleating calls attention to position in ponds and ditches. Feeds on ants, termites, slugs, spiders, and worms.
COLORADO RIVER TOAD *(Bufo alvarius)*	Dark brown or olive with smooth skin. Kidney-shaped parotoids and crests mark the head. Large warts on hind legs. Seven inches.	From Arizona to New Mexico and Southern California.	Although a desert animal, it is more aquatic than other toads and can be found in streams, irrigation ditches, and reservoirs. Feeds on insects, spiders, and lizards. Voice is low hoot.

Some Common Amphibians

NAME	DESCRIPTION	RANGE	HABITS
WESTERN TOAD (*Bufo boreas*)	Dusky with white stripe on back. No head crests. Parotoids oval in shape. Two to five inches.	Alaska to California. From Pacific to Rocky Mountains.	Commonly found in gardens. Also in desert streams, meadows, and woods. In warm parts of range, nocturnal; in colder parts, diurnal. Voice like that of baby chick.
OAK TOAD (*Bufo quercicus*)	Varicolored with many spots and stripes. Smallest U.S. toad; one inch.	From North Carolina to Louisiana.	Diurnal. Voice like bird peep. Found in pine woods.
SOUTHERN TOAD (*Bufo terrestris*)	Brown with high head crests that end in knobs. Two and a half inches.	Coastal Plain from Virginia to the Mississippi River.	In burrow by day; active at dusk and through night. Voice is high, pretty trill. Mating from March to September.

99

NAME	DESCRIPTION	RANGE	HABITS
FOWLER'S TOAD *(Bufo woodhousei fowleri)* formerly *B. fowleri*	Gray with irregular black or brown spots. Like American toad, but head crests and parotoids join, with no separation. Belly, smoothskinned and white, not spotted. Slim legs make for good jumping, Two to three inches.	New England to Louisiana, west to Michigan and Oklahoma.	Same gardens, meadows, ponds as American toad. Voice is eerie drone. Sometimes crossbreeds with American toad.
BARKING TREE FROG *(Hyla gratiosa)*	May be green, brown, or gray with round dark spots edged in black. Light stripe along sides. Stout body with granular skin. Tips of fingers and toes expanded into	Coastal Plain from North Carolina to Florida and Louisiana. (Introduced into New Jersey.)	Lives in tall trees, except during drought, when it burrows underground. Males have barking call. Very fine acrobat.

NAME	DESCRIPTION	RANGE	HABITS
	sucking discs. Two and a half inches.		
SQUIRREL TREE FROG *(Hyla squirella)*	Skin color changes from green to brown. May be spotted or plain. Thigh is yellow. Body is chunky. One and a half inches.	Virginia south through Florida and west to Texas.	Found high in trees as well as near human habitations. Makes sound like an angry squirrel. Eggs laid on pond bottom.
GREEN TREE FROG *(Hyla cinerea)*	Smooth skin is brilliant green, except in cool weather when it darkens. Sometimes has black-bordered golden spots on back. Longer legs than other tree frogs. Two and a half inches.	Delaware to Florida, west to Texas and north to Missouri and Illinois.	Found on stalks of weeds near ponds. During winter goes up into bushes away from water.

NAME	DESCRIPTION	RANGE	HABITS
SPRING PEEPER *(Hyla cruci-fer)*	Brown with dark cross on back. Body is translucent. Belly is white with yellow. Male has brown throat. One inch.	Common from Canada south throughout United States to Florida and Texas.	Sits on blades of grass near ponds. Call is shrill peeping that begins earliest of any frog — in March — and continues until May.
LITTLE GRASS FROG *(Hyla ocularis)*	Smallest of all U.S. frogs. Brown with dark line from eye to shoulder. One and a half inches.	Virginia south to Florida and west to Alabama.	Lives on low bushes or on grass in swamps. Able to turn head from side to side. Call sounds like insect chirp.
PACIFIC TREE FROG *(Hyla regilla)*	Color changes rapidly from clear tan or green to spotted and striped patterns with red, gold, and black showing. Sometimes bright, clear green. Two inches.	Canada through Southern California, east to Montana and Nevada.	Found from sea level to mountains. Breeds in marshes, ditches, reservoirs, and meadows. Usually found on ground among plants.

Some Common Amphibians

NAME	DESCRIPTION	RANGE	HABITS
CRICKET FROG (*Acris gryllus*)	Brown or gray with bright green stripe down back. Triangle on head. Belly white. One inch.	Eastern United States south to Florida and west to Texas, Kansas, and Northwest.	Leaps like cricket, but cannot climb trees. Lives in grass bordering ponds. Feeds on crickets, grasshoppers, insect larvae. Call is sharp chirp.
CHORUS FROG (*Pseudacris triseriata*)	Small brown frog without toe pads and little webbing. Dark stripe from snout to groin. White stripe on upper jaw. One-half to one and a half inches.	From Canada to Gulf of Mexico; New Jersey to Arizona.	Lives near pools, lakes, and marshes in flatlands and mountains. Frequently found near human habitations; even close to cities. Call sounds like whistle.

4. Your Own Amphibian

Reading a biography can give you a great deal of information about a man. You can learn about his ancestors, his home environment, and his way of life. You can even get an idea of the way he looks. But you will not know the man. The same is true of an animal. Through books you can find out about an animal's history, biology, and its living habits. But you will not understand that animal until you actually go out and meet it.

Meeting an amphibian is a relatively simple matter. You seek him out in places where he is likely to live at a time he is likely to be in evidence. The techniques for finding and observing amphibians are easy and you do not need any special equipment.

Amphibians can be found in every state in the United States. They do not live in the cities, for these are not likely to provide adequate living conditions. It is necessary to go a little way out to the country. There they will be in any moist, quiet situation.

When you meet an amphibian such as this bullfrog (*Rana catesbeiana*) on his own home ground, you have an opportunity to learn a great deal about him.

Before you leave on your expedition, stop and think for a moment. Just which kind of amphibian will you be searching for? Then use the information you have gathered to pick a suitable location in which to hunt. Is it an appropriate season for observing amphibians? Dry, hot days are likely to find all your potential aquaintances hiding underground or deep in the ponds. Cold winter days are suitable only for a few, very hardy species. Is the creature you are after lively during the day or does he put in an appearance only after dusk?

Once you have decided what to look for and where and when to find it, you will have to give a little thought to your personal needs while on the trip. Be sure to dress appropriately. Old, comfortable clothes are the best. Since most amphibians are at their best in damp weather, you had better plan to wear a raincoat. Early morning and late evening are likely to be chilly even during the summer, so if you plan to be out at those hours, wear a sweater. Be sure to wear comfortable shoes. You are not going to be able to drive right up to an amphibian to say hello. Some walking, perhaps a great deal of walking, is going to be necessary. If you are comfortable in water-resistant boots, wear them, for you will be on damp ground. Otherwise try roomy shoes that allow you maximum flexibility.

If you are planning an all-day trip, you had better provide yourself with some food. Take small, simple things, easy to carry in your pockets. Sandwiches, fruits, and nuts are all good. Bring along a canteen, for the pond you visit may not provide drinkable water.

You may be searching in the marshes for a favorite amphibian. If so, be sure to bring along some insect repellent. Mosquitoes can make a field trip a real misery.

Many amphibians are most easily observed at night. To see them, you will need a flashlight. Usually if you stand very still, the light will not bother them. You can shine it directly on your discovery and remain quiet. He will go right on about his business.

Once you have thought about your trip and are dressed and ready to go, get there as quickly as you can. Then slow down. Nobody ever discovered any wildlife by rushing. Remember that it may take you some time to find your quarry and if your pace is leisurely, you are less likely to tire.

This sort of marshland is the locale of many favorite amphibians.

Shouting and stomping will frighten away any little amphibian. Be quiet as you walk. Try not to brush against twigs or branches. Don't talk.

If you are going to meet an amphibian, you will have to find it first. Look carefully as you walk along. Get into the habit of turning over promising-looking rotten logs and moist rocks, without however destroying potential homes for many small animals. Listen for any possible calls.

Bring along a notebook, so you can quickly jot down information you will want later. If you make notes on each trip — when and where you went, what the weather was like, what species you saw — you will soon have a very good idea of how to plan subsequent trips for the utmost satisfaction.

When you get home from your trip, write yourself a detailed report from your notes. Include everything you have observed. Which species did you see? Was it breeding season? If so, make sure you write about any courtship activities you were able to witness. Also, what about actual mating? Were you able to find any eggs? Describe them. How were they attached? How many were there? If you are out in early summer, you will be lucky enough to see tadpoles and newly transformed adults. Note the differences between them and their parents. Find out what they eat. List everything you are able to observe about their daily habits. What are the effects of various weather conditions on a species? Have you noticed different sorts of amphibians in distinct natural situations? Which have you seen in meadows? Which in marshes? How does each amphibian react to danger?

Each trip you make will add more to your fund of information. Although it may be a little difficult at the beginning, after a few trips you will find yourself becoming more expert. Your work will be doubly rewarding. First, and most important, you will have established a real relationship with a charming group of animals. It will not be long before you will have figured out how to get a frog to eat from your hand, for instance. In addition to the warm feeling you will get from your friendship with amphibians, you may also find yourself the discoverer of a brand-new set of facts. For amphibians have been much neglected by scientists and very little is known about the habits of many species. Imagine the satisfaction you would feel at being the sole possessor of new knowledge about a favorite animal.

Visiting amphibians in their own natural homes is a delightful recreation. But perhaps you will decide to study one kind very seriously and at your leisure. Or you will simply fall in love with an amphibian and want it near you always. In either case, you are going to make a drastic change from objective observer to responsible owner. You must take your responsibility very seriously, for another life is involved. You are going to remove a living creature from its own choice of habitat to one of your own making.

Before you take an animal away from its natural environment, be prepared with a good substitute home. Since you have been watching carefully during your field trips, you will know what sort of conditions your creature has been accustomed to. You must try to duplicate them.

If you are interested in a serious study of amphibians, surely the best way to begin is with the animal's beginning — the egg. There are two ways to collect eggs. One is simply to go to the right pond during the breeding season and secure two adults about to mate. With frogs and toads, this is a relatively simple task. The male's song announces the time and place. So many individuals are there, that it will not take long to spot one male clasped onto a female's back in preliminary mating position. Because both animals are preoccupied with the task at hand, they do not exercise their usual caution with approaching strangers. Indeed, they will not even notice your presence.

Walk quietly up to the edge of the pond. Then begin to wade in slowly for a few feet. When you have located your prey through sound and then flashlight beam, catch them in your hand (or use a net if you prefer), and dump them into a canvas bag for transporting. Fill a gallon jar with water from the pond and add a few of the water plants. As soon as you get home, place the pair into the jar or an aquarium full of their own pond water and plants. There is an excellent chance that they will go right on with their mating. You will then have their fertilized eggs in your possession. Keep only a few of them. Scoop out the rest in some of the water and put their parents back in the bag. Return them all to the pond where you found them.

The most direct way to collect eggs is simply to find out where they have been laid and take a few. Most salamanders attach their eggs to water plants. Frog eggs are frequently found in gelatinous masses, floating on the surface of a pond, while those of toads are in long, beadlike strings at the bottom. If you have been doing your nature observing efficiently, you will know just where to look for the kind of egg you want.

Once you have some amphibian eggs in your own home, you can sit back and watch the action. The next few days will be fascinating. You need do nothing for the eggs. Their needs are met with the water and plants you have already provided. This would be a good time to prepare a home for the prospective larvae.

While the tadpoles are little, you can go on keeping them in your jar. If you are going to keep a lot of them, however, you will need a larger home. The aquarium tank is probably your best bet. In order to provide enough oxygen for your amphibians, you need a large surface of water exposed to the air. It is better to have a wide, shallow tank than a deep, narrow one. If you intend to buy a tank in a pet store, look for one with a metal frame, as it is sturdier than the all-glass type. With a large number of tadpoles, you will do better with several small tanks rather than one large tank.

Small tanks are easy to make and you might prefer that to buying them. You will need six panes of glass — four of them 8″ x 10″ and two 8″ x 8″. You will also need a roll of 2″ adhesive tape. Fasten the four side pieces together with the adhesive tape (two of the 8 x 10's and two 8 x 8's). Then attach the bottom with more tape. Add a second layer of tape to the bottom and line the edges of the top of the case with tape. Use the sixth piece of glass as a lid. You need not attach it, but should line the edges of it with tape. When you have finished putting it together, you might like to paint the tape a cheerful color. The inside corners should be puttied with aquarium cement. If you intend to move your tank around frequently, set it on a wooden base, slightly larger than the tank.

Whether you buy your aquarium or build it, you must test it for watertightness before using it. Fill it with water and let it stand overnight. If, in the morning, you find that it has leaked, you will need to repair it with cement.

When you are looking for a good permanent position for the tank, keep in mind that the temperature should be constant (about 60° is ideal for amphibians, so avoid radiators). Steady sunlight is important, so a position not too distant from a window with a good northern exposure is ideal. You can solve any lighting problem with electricity. An electric bulb or an aquarium reflector can be placed above the tank.

Tadpoles are easy to feed. You can simply scoop out some algae from any stagnant pond. This will satisfy their needs until their mouths are transformed and working. Frog and toad larvae are vegetarians and you can feed them with small quantities of cooked lettuce. All tadpoles do well on corn meal. This is probably the simplest of all foods, for you have only to sprinkle a little in the water each day. Since tadpoles are natural scavengers, they will clean up their own tank, if not overfed. If you see bits of food remaining by the next feeding, however, you must get it out before it has time to foul the water. A small dip tube works well in removing any debris. Just put your finger over one end of the tube and lower the other end to the bottom of the tank. Raise your finger and the water with the debris will fill the tube. Put your finger back over the open end and lift the tube and its contents out for dumping.

Salamander larvae will feed on corn meal, too, but the best food is insects and insect larvae. In order to keep a steady supply, you may want to raise some yourself. Aquatic insects can be raised in a glass jar. Put a layer of sand on the bottom of the jar and fill with pond water. Add a small cutting from a water plant, with part of the plant above water level. Cover the jar with a piece of screening. If you have vegetarian insects, that is all they will need. If you are raising meat-eaters, you will have to add small insect life that you scoop from ponds with a dip net.

A meat bone added to a salamander larvae tank will provide a great occasional treat.

If the sides of your tank become caked with green slime and the water looks green as well, don't worry about it too much. This is just algae growing. It won't hurt your tadpoles at all. It might make it difficult for you to view, however, so you will probably decide to get rid of it. Since it is sunlight that causes algae to grow, the simplest solution is to move the tank to a somewhat darker situation. To hurry the clearing procedure, you might also want to scrape the sides with a razor blade. To keep it clean and neat, add a few pond snails to your tank. They will multiply in time, but don't worry — your amphibians will soon mature to the stage where snail meat tastes good.

Careful selection of a position for your aquarium, the addition of the right sort of plants, and scrupulous cleaning of debris pays a dividend. You will never have to change the water. The glass top will keep evaporation down. Just lift it slightly (a matchbook under one corner is sufficient) to allow air to enter. Add a little water occasionally to keep the level constant, but do not use tap water, unless you have set it aside for twenty-four hours to allow sufficient time for

Your terrarium should provide a home similar to your pet's native habitat.

114

the chlorine to disappear. You can buy anti-chlorine mixture at your pet store for immediate decontamination.

In time, your tadpoles will begin their fascinating process of metamorphosis. You will need to prepare for this. Put in a flat rock that projects just above water level, or float a piece of wood on top of the water. If tadpoles are forced to remain in the water at the time their lungs take on the job of breathing, they may drown. Once they have come out of the water, you will have to transfer those that are land-living.

Making a permanent home for adult amphibians is the real test of your ability as a naturalist. You must remember where you saw adults of this species in the wild and do your utmost to duplicate those conditions.

If your pet is one of the woodland amphibians (a toad, for instance), you can plan a home that will be comfortable for him and beautiful for anyone observing. Go back to the woods where you saw others of his kind. Take with you a sturdy box and a few plastic bags. A newspaper is also handy. You will need digging tools — a small spade and your pocket-knife should do nicely. Look first for some nice clumps of moss. Take them up carefully in long sheets. Put them down in the bottom of the box and cover them with some newspaper.

Now look around for some pretty, small plants. Use your trowel to dig beneath them and make sure you take the whole root along with some of the earth surrounding it. Place each plant in some newspaper and wrap it gently. Put the plants, individually wrapped, on top of the moss. Don't try to transplant anything exotic. Some of the prettiest plants are also the hardiest and these are the ones to use. Pack some nice-looking pieces of bark and a few small rocks. Use the paper bags for carrying plenty of the good, rich leaf mold under your feet.

115

Hurry home and be ready to plant immediately. The bottom of your tank should be covered with a two-inch layer of gravel or pebbles, mixed with a few bits of charcoal. Now add two inches of leaf mold. This should be moistened enough so that it will form a ball in your hand when you squeeze it. Then add your rocks, placing them in interesting positions in the tank. Arrange your plants as naturally as you can, placing the taller ones nearer the back. Finally, take your carefully preserved sheets of moss and set them down like a carpet around the base of your plants. Tap the moss down very gently. Add any sticks, pebbles, and bark you feel will enhance the effect.

Moisten the planted tank evenly (a small sprinkling can works best) and place it in a cool spot. Keep it shaded, as the woods are. If you keep the glass cover on the tank, you will not need to do any further watering. If you should notice a lot of moisture on the sides, use a matchstick under the cover. This will raise it just enough to allow the excess moisture to evaporate. Remove the stick when the moisture has disappeared.

Suppose your amphibian is one of the many that makes its home in the swamps. You will then want to provide a bog terrarium.

The first thing to do is to make sure your tank is completely watertight. Then provide for two separate areas — one will be land and the other water. Get a piece of glass about half as high as the sides of the tank and place it as a divider between the two sections. You can fasten it in place with a little aquarium cement. Proceed with the land side as you would for a woodland terrarium. Two inches of gravel, mixed with charcoal for sweetening, is your bottom layer. Dig up some sphagnum moss from the nearest marsh to provide a three-inch layer that comes next. Get it very wet.

116

If the water portion of your tank is deep enough, you will be able to observe the position of your pet while swimming. In nature, you would see nothing but the eyes and nostrils of this leopard frog (*Rana pipiens*).

While you are out digging bog plants for the terrarium, be sure to take along plenty of rich soil from around them for the third layer of the tank. Note the depth of the plant roots as you dig, so that you can transplant them properly. You can add a few small rocks or a piece of rotting tree branch to the top.

Over on the water side, you will need to provide a bank for your creature to use in moving from one side to the other. Pile some earth and pebbles against the glass partition. Fill the rest with marsh water and a few aquatic plants and you will have duplicated the natural habitat of most common amphibians.

All amphibians need a bit of privacy, so be sure to provide a hiding place of some sort. A little cave made of rocks would be fine. A flowerpot, placed sideways, works just as well.

Burrowing animals, which need a lot of privacy, do not make the best pets. But if you have an interest in that sort of amphibian, you can keep it in a large glass jar. Wrap some black paper around the sides. Fill the jar with sandy soil. When you have put the animal inside, cover the jar and leave it alone for a time. When the burrower has had a chance to get used to its new surroundings, you may remove the black paper and see what he is doing. Be sure to replace the paper after each observation, or your pet will be most uncomfortable.

Some amphibians remain aquatic all their lives. Use the same sort of arrangement as you would for tadpoles, not neglecting the floating perch. An aquatic situation is a little harder to keep clean, so don't put in a lot of accessories. The less cluttered the tank, the easier it is to clean.

In keeping amphibian pets, there are several important considerations. First of all, be sure you do not overcrowd your tank. Two or three occupants to a medium-sized tank is enough. Make sure you include only animals of the same size or else the largest is likely to have the smaller ones for dinner. Use your space wisely. Different kinds of amphibians in one tank, rather than several of one habit, make for more room and greater interest. For instance, you can put tree

Be sure to include a hiding place, such as this flowerpot, in your amphibian's tank. Shown here is a marine toad (*Bufo marinus*).

119

frogs into the same tank in which you have toads. The tree frogs will stay up in the plants, while the toads squat on the ground.

Don't overfeed. Remember, however, that even the tiniest tadpole will grow to be a large adult with an insatiable appetite for insects. If it is going to be difficult for you to find enough of these, then keep away from the larger species.

Watching a pet feed is a great pleasure. Be careful, however, not to overfeed your amphibian. This Mexican tree frog (*Smilisca baudini*) is about to flip out its tongue.

You can eliminate the feeding problem by growing your own food. Earthworms are a big hit with many adult amphibians. You can start an earthworm culture in a wooden crate. Fill it with about one inch of moist soil. Buy or dig up as many earthworms as you can. The box will hold well over a hundred. Place the worms on the soil and cover them with a layer of rotting leaves. Feed them with corn meal, breadcrumbs, or cooked vegetables once or twice a week. Be sure to keep the soil moist but not wet. You can cut down on evaporation by covering the container. A sheet of glass or an old piece of heavy cloth will do nicely. Keep the box in a cool, shaded indoor place. (The basement is ideal.) You can also buy earthworms at many pet stores and bait shops.

White worms are fine for smaller amphibians. You can buy some at a pet store and let them propagate. Set them into the same sort of situation suggested for raising earthworms, but add cooked vegetables and meat rather than rotting leaves. White worms *(Enchytraeus)* are much too small to be picked up individually for feeding. Simply scoop up a clump of an appropriate size when you need them.

Mealworms are another favorite amphibian food. These are actually the larvae of certain beetles and not true worms at all. You can buy a culture from a nearby pet store. Fill a glass jar with bran and crumple a paper towel on top of the bran. On the paper, place a chunk of apple or potato. Now dump in your culture, which should include adults, eggs, and larvae. Cover the jar with window screening and leave it in a warm place. When the apple or potato dries out, replace it. Mealworms are inexpensive and easily available, so you may not want to go to the trouble of raising them. If you are going to buy them from the pet store for feeding, be sure not to waste your money by getting more than a few days' supply. Do not feed your pets exclusively on mealworms, for they are constipating.

Crickets are easy to raise and provide the healthiest sort of amphibian diet.

Perhaps the healthiest food for amphibians is crickets. Most pet stores sell them. You could raise them yourself. Start with a glass jar or aquarium tank. Put down a two-inch layer of soil and cover with some screening. Add a small water dish. Feed the crickets moistened bread, mashed potatoes, and lettuce. Sprinkle the crickets with some powdered vitamins for a truly nourishing meal.

122

Fruit flies are good food for many tiny amphibians, tree frogs particularly. You can gather fruit flies easily by leaving a little decaying fruit in a bottle near the window. Scientists have developed a strain without wings for easy care at home. You can buy a culture in some pet stores or through biological supply houses. The same source will supply the medium on which they feed. Put some of this into a wide-mouthed jar. Add a crumpled paper towel and a few fruit flies. Then plug the bottle up with some cotton. In about two weeks, you will have more fruit flies than you ever dreamed possible.

Small fish make good food for aquatic types. You can find minnows being sold at many bait shops and guppies in all pet stores. Guppies are easy to raise at home and multiply faster than your amphibians can eat. Just buy a pair (you can recognize the males by their smaller size and bigger tail), and put them in a small tank filled with dechlorinated water and a plant or two. You do not really need any special equipment, but if you want quick results, buy an aquarium heater and a light and feed them lots of fish flakes. In a short time, you will see innumerable tiny guppies near the bottom of the tank. If you take just a few at a time, soon the babies will have babies, etc., etc. You will have a constant supply of food as well as another pleasant and instructive pet community.

If you are looking for an easy supply of food for your tadpoles, you can buy infusoria tablets at your local pet store. Infusoria is a name given to many different kinds of microscopic plants and animal cells appetizing to young frogs and toads. The tablets sold at stores can be dropped directly into the water in your tank. (One a day is more than adequate for a medium-sized tank with several larvae.) As the tablet dissolves, food is released for the infusoria, which will then rapidly multiply.

123

Pet stores carry other foods acceptable to many amphibians. Tubifex worms are available almost everywhere and are eaten by many aquatic salamanders. These worms resemble tiny wiggling earthworms that stay clumped together in water. Do not buy more than three or four days' supply, for the worms will not live longer than that and the salamander is not interested in dead worms. Put in just enough to satisfy your pet at one meal. Too many in the tank will foul the water. The worms can be kept in a closed container in the refrigerator between feedings.

Freeze-dried tubifex worms are packaged in small cubes. You can break off an appropriate-sized piece and throw it into the water in your tank. As the cube dissolves, the tiny dead worms separate and float free. Many salamanders and newts will dine on these worms. Some will also accept dried tropical fish food.

During the warm seasons of the year, many insects are available to you. You have simply to step outdoors and catch them. Beetles, moths, flies, grasshoppers, and dragonflies all make good eating. Most household pests can be put to use as amphibian fodder. Just dump into your tank any houseflies, moths, or roaches you encounter and you will have solved two problems simultaneously. If you have a plant covered with plant lice, just put the pot into the terrarium and watch your pet do a clean job on the plant.

Of course, it is best to feed any pet with the food it would find in nature. But sometimes this is inconvenient or even impossible. If you are very patient you can teach an amphibian to accept other food. Lean meat is nourishing for most amphibians. Frogs and toads accept only moving food, however, so you must make it move. Take a small piece of meat and tie it to the end of a long line of string. Dangle it right in front of you pet's eyes and let him jump up and catch it.

Repeat until his appetite is sated. Be careful not to stand where you throw a shadow over your pet or jiggle too violently, for he will be too frightened to eat.

It is important to keep your pet's diet varied. Do not limit him to one or two foods, as it may lead to digestive disorders.

A few good foods are listed below:

THE SPOTTED SALAMANDER — small crustaceans and tubifex worms.

NEWTS — lean beef. They will also accept small bits of fish and liver.

CRICKET FROGS — fruit flies and small mealworms.

THE GREEN TREE FROG — houseflies.

BULLFROGS have enormous appetites and will eat anything that moves. Always keep a bullfrog in solitary confinement.

MUD PUPPIES need one or two big feedings weekly — raw beefsteak, strips of beef liver, or hunks of fresh fish as a substitute for the foods they naturally eat.

Earthworms are suitable for almost all amphibians.

You should be able to prevent most amphibian diseases with proper care. Of particular importance are: a clean, well-planned tank with a cool, constant temperature; uncrowded conditions within the tank; a varied diet in appropriate quantities. (Overfeeding is more harmful than underfeeding.)

There is always some danger of illness, however, even when you have been very careful. If one of your pets is afflicted, you are going to have to make some serious decisions. If you have several animals in one tank, you must separate the one that is diseased as soon as you observe the first symptoms. Most amphibian ailments are contagious and will spread throughout the entire tank. Also, if you want to try to cure your sick pet, lots of special attention must be

If a pet becomes ill, it is always wise to isolate him immediately. Here is a leopard frog (*Rana pipiens*) in quarantine.

devoted to the job and that is easier if he is separately housed. Be forewarned, though. Many amphibian ailments are almost impossible to cure in a terrarium situation.

The kindest and least frustrating course to follow is to return your sick pet to his natural environment. This is also true with the problem-eater. If, after several days, an amphibian refuses food, return him to the spot where you found him. No one wants to watch a pet deliberately starve himself to death.

Several of the most common amphibian ailments are listed below, primarily to enable you to recognize the symptoms.

126

Methods of treatment are also given, although cure is always doubtful.

Salamanders have extremely delicate skin. It is easily damaged and this leads to very serious illnessess. Be careful to avoid scratching or bruising when transporting your pet. Be sure not to put two or more aggressive males into the same tank, for skin injuries incurred during a battle can be fatal.

If you notice patches of white fuzz on your salamander, you will know that his skin has been hurt and a fungus infection has started. This fungus is highly contagious and will

Salamanders have very delicate skin. Great care must be exercised not to bruise or scratch your pet or serious disease may follow. Shown here is a northwestern salamander (*Ambystoma gracile*).

spread quickly to contaminate the other occupants of the tank if you do not take immediate steps to prevent this. Separate the sick animal from the others. Put him in one tank and the others in another. The tank in which they have been living must be completely cleaned and sterilized before re-using. Everything — gravel, plants, and rocks — must be re-moved and carefully washed. The tank itself must be thoroughly scoured before it is safe to place another am-phibian into it.

A pet store proprietor might suggest potassium permanga-nate for fungus infections. This is definitely not a remedy for amphibians. Many people believe that dipping the diseased animal into a salt-water solution will help, but it will not. The salamander with the fungus infection should be placed in a situation with running water. Should this prove difficult in your home, be sure to change the water in the tank at frequent intervals through the day.

Some antibiotics have been used successfully in treating salamander skin diseases. Your local veterinarian can prescribe the right kinds. You must also find out from him the correct dosage for your pet (it is determined by the animal's weight), for it will be up to you to administer the medication. Do not, under any circumstances, allow your amphibian to receive injections.

Salamander "leprosy" is the name given to a horrible disease with symptoms resembling those of human leprosy. The animal appears swollen with bloody splotches beneath the skin. The skin turns dull, shrinks, and then peels. The peeled areas seep moisture. The tips of the tail and the digits begin to rot. The salamander has no appetite.

This unsightly condition appears to be due to overcrowd-ing and generally unclean, overly dry terrarium conditions. Potassium permanganate and sulfa powders are not effective.

The disease is almost hopeless. But antibiotics are sometimes helpful and should be tried if you are fond of your pet. You must also place him in a clean, empty tank with a lid. Do not put any gravel on the bottom of the aquarium. Add just a half inch of water and a small rock for climbing. Slant your tank slightly by putting a matchbook under one end. Spray it daily with a little clean dechlorinated water.

Sometimes swellings under the skin can be caused by heart and kidney diseases. They might even be a symptom of tubercular disorder. If so, you can offer a little relief by puncturing the swollen areas and draining the fluid.

Skin swellings in salamanders can be the result of constipation. Watch your pet carefully to see if he is eliminating regularly. When you are sure that constipation is the source of the problem, force feed cod liver oil. Do not offer any food until the animal has resumed normal elimination. Gently massage the swollen area.

Should your salamander begin to demonstrate difficulty in swallowing, you will know that he has a sore throat. Put him into a low-water situation or lay him on a little clump of moss. Allow him to rest quietly in isolation until he has recovered.

Eye and lid diseases are frequent and always quite noticeable. The affected area looks sore and swollen. Place the afflicted animal in an antibiotic solution for an almost sure cure. Keep spraying him with fresh water.

Roundworms are parasites that can cause salamanders a lot of discomfort. They are quite noticeable in the stool. If your animal has begun to lose weight rapidly in spite of feeding well, check carefully for any small white worms crawling in his excrement. If they are there, remove all the gravel in the tank immediately. You must either disinfect the old gravel with boiling salt water or get some new gravel. Change the water frequently, force feed some cod liver oil, and hope for the best.

Adult males frequently become belligerent toward one another in captivity. Sometimes they fight so ferociously that they severely damage legs and tails. If your pets suffer such wounds, it is wise to amputate the affected parts. The tails will regenerate (grow back) and a missing leg will scarcely be noticed by your pet.

One of the most serious illnesses to which frogs and toads are prone occurs when they are very young. This is rickets, a disease of the bones that troubles many rapidly growing young creatures, including humans. You can prevent this by offering lots of vitamins. This will be an easy matter if crickets are the main source of food. You simply sprinkle your culture with a liberal dose of a powdered vitamin preparation at frequent intervals. Bone meal is good too. It won't bother the crickets — they'll simply be covered with powder — and your young pets will be protected without knowing it.

Frogs and toads also suffer from roundworms. Detection is easier than with salamanders, for one of the first symptoms is a yellowing of the iris. Use the same treatment recommended for salamanders.

Occasionally, you will notice a toad with a nose that appears to be rotting. Some blowfly has managed to lay its eggs there and the larvae have hatched. You should drip a disinfectant (like Lysol) on the larvae and try to remove them with tweezers.

Frogs also get "leprosy" and need the same isolation and treatment recommended for salamanders.

Aquatic frogs can develop cramps and even paralysis if the tank is allowed to remain dirty. Hurry up and clean it.

Paralysis can also be caused by a lack of calcium. Douse

some crickets with powdered calcium or bone meal and add a dash of vitamims A and D, while you are about it.

Tree frogs are frequently troubled by constipation. An unfortunate symptom is an everted rectum. (It sticks out rather than remaining inward.) Feed your pet plenty of cod liver oil. The rectum may or may not return to its normal position when the condition has been relieved.

One of the most frequent diseases of aquatic frogs is "red leg." It is caused by an airborne bacterium and can happen anywhere. As suggested by the name of the disease, the major symptom is a red flush that appears on the hind legs. It also colors most of the underparts of the afflicted animal. The redness is caused by the breaking up of blood vessels just beneath the skin. The kidneys are affected and cannot properly eliminate all the fluid taken in the skin. The body becomes bloated. The condition is very serious, but can often be checked with antibiotics.

The pickerel frog *(Rana palustris)* has a skin secretion that is absolutely fatal to all other frogs. There is no cure. Just be sure to keep this frog in a separate tank.

Administering medicine to a sick amphibian is a little complicated. You must be sure not to injure him more with the treatment than he has been with the illness. The best method is to put the prescribed dosage into an eyedropper. You can buy one that is marked along the sides for proper measuring. Attach the end of the eyedropper to a thin rubber tube. The insulation referred to as "rubber spaghetti" that covers electric wires, works well for this purpose. Slice the end of the tube at an angle. Then gently slip the tube deep into the animal's throat and squeeze the bulb of the eyedropper.

Frogs can get very nervous in captivity. They may fling themselves against the sides and lid of the tank. In so doing, they frequently injure themselves. Eye wounds can be treated with antibiotics dropped directly into the eye. Bruised noses just have to heal by themselves. If these nervous habits continue after the animal has been in your home for several days, it is kind to release him.

After you have kept some of the local kinds of amphibians, you may want to try your hand at some more exotic species. Pet stores carry a dazzling variety of imported frogs and salamanders. Some are very beautiful. Many have fascinating living habits. When you consider yourself an expert, buy one. Do not do so before you have considerable experience, for if you are unsuccessful, or find you haven't the time to devote to your hobby, you will not be able to release the animal. If you put an amphibian native to one area into an alien environment, you are almost certainly condemning him to death and may be making serious problems for the local inhabitants besides.

Before buying an amphibian from another part of the world, check carefully with the pet store owner as to its needs and home conditions. Use your discretion when listening to the answers. Many pet store owners are knowledgeable and sincere, but some do not know the answers and others will not tell anything that might hinder a sale. This is when your own experience and common sense will help. Do a little extra reading about the area from which the amphibian was taken and find out what the climate is and what kinds of food he is likely to have found. If it can't be duplicated by you, think of a logical substitute.

Check to be sure the animal you select is healthy. Pick the fattest, most active animal in the tank. Make sure the eyes are clear and shiny. The body should be perfect with well-formed tail and limbs and a full complement of toes. Be particularly critical of the skin. Any trace of white fuzz eliminates not only the animal that carries it, but the others in that tank.

When you have your amphibian home, you may find that he is unwilling to eat. This is not an unusual circumstance with exotic amphibians. Allow him a few days to become adjusted to his new surroundings. Then, if he is still refusing food, you will have to force feed him. Use some raw, lean beef and ground-up insects mixed into a solution of cod liver oil. Feed with the medicine eyedropper described above. After a while your pet should begin to take food by himself.

A few of the most spectacular foreign species available in pet stores are described here:

The Axolotl
(Ambystoma mexicanum)

This Mexican native is one of the most popular pet store amphibians. Although it is quite different in appearance, it is closely related to the tiger salamander *(Ambystoma tigrinum)* found in the United States. Axolotls are permanently larval, with prominent gills. They have funny, clownlike faces which appear to be constantly smiling. Frequently pet stores carry albino specimens, which are highly prized by amphibian fanciers.

In nature, axolotls live in cold highland lakes. To keep them in their neotenic state, you must provide deep, cool water or they may metamorphose and become ordinary salamanders.

133

The Giant Salamander
(*Megalobatrachus japonicus*)

This large amphibian is related to the North American hellbender (*Cryptobranchus alleganiensis*). Both belong to the family Cryptobranchidae. Like the hellbender, the giant salamander is a completely aquatic animal of large proportions and appetites. In its native streams high in the mountains of Japan, it feeds on fish, worms, insects, and other salamanders. The people of Japan fish for these large salamanders eagerly, for it is a good source of protein and is considered very tasty, besides.

It may be a little difficult to find in pet stores. Some do stock them, though, from time to time and they do well in captivity. There are records of giant salamanders who have lived for over fifty years in carefully tended aquariums. Remember, however, that this animal reaches a length of over five feet and requires a lot of food and a very large tank.

The Smooth Newt
(*Triturus vulgaris*)

This European newt belongs to the family Salamandridae, which includes the newts of the United States as well as several other Old World species. The crested or warty newt (*Triturus cristatus*) is a larger European species frequently encountered in pet stores.

All newts make lovely pets, but the male smooth newt is particularly beautiful, especially during the breeding season. A large crest develops along the back and the tail sports a frilly fin. Both are edged in brilliant red.

If you are lucky enough to get a pair of smooth newts and would like to have them mate, be sure to put them into a tank with both water and land situations. For although smooth newts are terrestrial most of the time, they become completely aquatic at the breeding season. Courtship is elaborate and involved. Young newts are charming. Any difficulty you might have in setting up a comfortable home will be more than adequately rewarded.

The Japanese Newt
(Cynops pyrrhogaster)

Although imported from the Orient, this is probably the most common pet store amphibian. Certainly it is the easiest newt to raise. It feeds well and is extremely hardy. It is not the least bit shy. A Japanese newt can live for years in captivity, given just a minimum of thought and consideration. Raw meat is accepted greedily, so no special food problem need arise. In no time, you can have it eating from your hand.

The Japanese newt has most attractive coloring; its back is black and it has a bright red belly. Even if you have not had the opportunity to observe and collect domestic species, you can safely and easily raise this foreigner.

The Fire Salamander
(Salamandra salamandra)

Fire salamanders belong to the newt family Salamandridae, but are not nearly as hardy as other members of the group. They are particularly susceptible to fungus diseases, which can sometimes be cured with great patience and skill. No novice should undertake their care, however. For the expert, the fire salamander is an interesting and worthwhile pet. It has a graceful body covered with bright yellow markings against a dark background.

Many extraordinary superstitions have grown around this small animal. The theory that it is born of the flames of a fire gives it its name. Perhaps another factor leading to the naming of this amphibian is the burning sensation any predator will feel if it should bite into a fire salamander, for there is a poisonous skin secretion.

The Amphiuma
(Amphiuma)

One of the most unusual of all salamanders is found in the United States. The entire family Amphiumidae is made up of just the single genus *Amphiuma*. It is found naturally in the southeastern section of the country.

Amphiumas look more like eels than salamanders. The tiny legs and arms can be seen, but only if looked for. They usually live among swampy water weeds, where their grayish-brown color blends well and provides camouflage for their rather large bodies. Amphiumas are able to squirm along on land and they lay their eggs above water level in small nests. The female stays near at hand to guard her brood.

Amphiumas will eat insects, fish, crayfish, and snails. Although you are unlikely to provide it, they will also take as food small snakes and frogs.

There are three species of amphiumas, each named for the number of digits per limb: the three-toed amphiuma, the two-toed amphiuma, and the one-toed amphiuma.

Be very careful when handling an amphiuma. It is one of

the few really aggressive salamanders. With their sharp teeth and strong jaws, they can bite hard enough to hurt.

The Surinam Toad
(Pipa pipa)

The Surinam toad is one of a family of peculiar amphibians (the Pipidae) without tongues. Sometimes the group is referred to as the Aglossa, which means tongueless.

Surinam toads are not pretty. They are short and broad and flat as a pancake. They are overall a dark brown color, with odd flaps of skin along the jaws. All this works well to disguise these toads as they glide along the mud in their native rivers, the Amazon and the Orinoco, but it does not add much to their allure in an aquarium. The Surinam toad does not even have, as a redeeming feature, the lovely eyes that characterize most tailless amphibians. The eyes are tiny, beadlike, and solid black.

Although this amphibian will not add beauty to your tank, it will provide interest. You will enjoy watching it feed, for it does not catch its prey in the usual frog manner. The aquatic Surinam toad sweeps through the mud with its long, sensitive fingers to grab any small animal (dead or alive) that may be hidden there. Then, fanning the water around the prey, the toad swishes it up into its gaping mouth.

In the water, the Surinam toad is quick and surprisingly graceful for so awkward-looking an animal.

These amphibians do well in captivity and you should have no hesitancy in adding them to your collection. You might even be lucky enough to get a pair to mate. In that case, you will be in for an exciting experience. *Pipa pipa* has special provisions for nesting. The female has pockets on her back

137

for the carrying of eggs and, as the male fertilizes each one, he shifts it onto the female's back. After a few hours, the skin on the back swells and covers the egg, making the mother look quite fat. The young remain in their cells until metamorphosis is complete, and appear, finally, as tiny but perfect Surinam toads.

To keep such young amphibians alive, it is wise to remove the parents from the tank soon after they make their debut.

Surinam toads will eat almost anything. They do especially well on small pieces of lean beef.

The Clawed Frog
(*Xenopus laevis*)

Another tongueless frog is the well-known clawed frog of Africa. It is well suited to life in an aquarium, taming easily and eating ravenously. The clawed frog can be purchased in almost any pet store, quite inexpensively. You need only the simplest aquarium tank to house it. Do not add the clawed frog to a fish tank, for it will rapidly consume all your prize specimens.

Pet stores sell young clawed frogs at the time when they look most appealing. Tiny, delicate little creatures, they seem, with their birdlike claws on the three inner toes of the hind feet. But in a very short time, they grow to be large, grotesque amphibians, looking much like carelessly made stuffed toys.

Clawed frogs use the fingers of their front legs for pushing food into their mouths. They also use them, along with their sharp, clawed toes, for catching prey.

Purchase one or two clawed frogs for amusement, for they are fun to watch, but be sure to keep them in a separate tank. Do not bother with a pretty, decorative aquarium, for they will soon tear it apart with their violent movements. Be careful to keep the temperature of the water constant; 65° to 75° is best.

The Fire-bellied Toad
(*Bombina bombina*)

Unless you startle him, this small (about 2″) amphibian looks quite dull and colorless. When frightened, however, he will roll over quickly, draw his legs up, and begin to writhe. Then you will see the brilliant orange spots that give him his name. This behavior scares off most predators. Do not count on its occurrence too often in your tank, though, for the fire-belly learns fast just who his friends are and will stop trying to threaten you as soon as he begins to associate you with meals.

Fire-bellies belong to the family Discoglossidae, whose members all have round, disclike tongues that cannot be distended in normal frog fashion. The genus *Bombina* is found in Europe and Asia in swampland, so try a marsh terrarium. Fire-bellies can also be raised in an aquarium, if you plant some aquatic foliage. They will eat raw beef nicely, but you can also give them a housefly or two.

These toads have a poisonous skin secretion in addition to their protective coloring, so they are rarely troubled by other animals. When you handle them, be careful to wash your hands afterward.

The voice of the fire-bellied toad is a low, melancholy croak. Your pet will sing to you all year long, particularly when he notices you nearby.

Horned Frogs
(genus Ceratophrys)

The horned frogs of South America belong to a family (Leptodactylidae) in which the members do not resemble each other too closely. Genera can be found in the West Indies, in tropical America, and in Australia. Several species of the genus *Ceratophrys* are native to South America.

Horned frogs are fun to keep as pets, for they are ridiculously aggressive. They will charge at an owner who is trying to feed them long past the time when they should have learned better. If you decide to buy one of these, you had better buy some long-handled forceps as well. Feeding is never going to be friendly. You will certainly have bruised fingers if you try to do it by hand.

Although their huge mouths and strong jaws would indicate that these frogs should take large prey, they are quite satisfied with beetles, cockroaches, and earthworms.

The "horn" is not made up of hard, bony substance, but is simply an extra flap of skin that protrudes above each eye. This makes the head seem quite enormous and that fact, coupled with the frog's belligerent behavior, frightens away other animals.

There are several species of horned frogs varying greatly in size and color. Some reach a length of eight inches, while other species are barely one inch long.

All are great fun in a terrarium, when kept singly and providing you are not hoping for affection from your pet.

The Giant Toad
(Bufo marinus)

This large (9″) true toad makes its home throughout most of tropical America. It can be found in South America, Central America, Mexico, and even in the southern portion of Texas. It has been introduced by man into several other tropical areas because of its value as a killer of sugar-plantation pests.

The large size of the giant toad allows it to eat many animals unavailable to other amphibians. In addition to sugar beetles, therefore, it will also consume small vertebrates, such as mice. It does not seem to matter whether it grabs its prey at the hind or front end, when eating. A rather amazing fact when you consider that rodents have sharp teeth.

The giant toad will eat well for you in captivity. It makes a nice pet. Its intelligence is superior to that of most amphibians and it is a highly responsive friend. If you will place a small pool of water in its tank, the giant toad will sit luxuriously to soak for hours, although it does not actively swim at all. You will need a very large tank to keep him healthy and lots of fresh food daily.

Arrow-poison Frogs
(genus Dendrobates)

Deep in the forests of Central and South America live a group of tiny frogs who carry a skin secretion so poisonous that they have become notorious for it. Long ago, before white men ever came to tropical America, the Indians knew of the virulent effects of this animal's secretion. They would spear a small frog with a sharp stick and then dangle it above a fire. The heat would cause the skin glands to sweat and drops of poison that fell would be carefully gathered into a container. The drops were left to ferment for a while before the hunters' arrows were dipped into the fluid. These poison-tipped arrows, when shot into a small mammal or bird, caused immediate paralysis.

You will suffer no such effect, should you decide to keep one of these dramatically colored little frogs, but perhaps it would be wise to avoid handling it as much as possible. If it is necessary for you to touch this pet, wash your hands carefully afterward.

All dendrobates are tiny, beautiful creatures. Some are black with shiny blue spots; others are green or pink with black spots. There are those with bright yellow stripes. Perhaps the most gorgeous is the golden arrow-poison frog of Central America with its metallic sheen of bronze.

Zetek's Frog
(*Atelopus zeteki*)

This handsome frog is one of an unusual group that belongs to the family Atelopodidae. There is just one genus (*Atelopus*), but numerous species that are scattered widely over most of South America and sections of Central America as well. Some of these frogs have sharp noses like that of Zetek's frog, but others have square heads with flat snouts. Some members have no inner toes and the three outer toes are fused into a single long claw. In all of them, the coloring is magnificent.

Zetek's frog (*Atelopus zeteki*).

Zetek's frog is the best-looking of the lot with black spots dramatically opposed to its golden-yellow back. It comes from Panama, where it cavorts by day on rocks near and in streams. It can be easily spotted with its brilliant color, but it is protected by the toxicity of its skin. It has no natural enemies.

Zetek's frog is not nervous, so it will not be alarmed by you as its keeper. Gentle handling will discourage any secretion.

The Golden Tree Frog
(*Hyla aurea*)

All the tree frogs make charming pets. Most feed well in captivity and respond nicely to their owners. The golden tree frog of Australia is one of the larger members of the group, reaching a length of about three inches. It has a pleasantly round appearance and lovely color. The back is bright emerald green with the golden stripe running along the sides. Its disposition is gentle and it tames easily.

The footpads of a golden tree frog are smaller and not as well developed as those of other members of the family. This amphibian lives in the low bushes surrounding a pond. A marshland terrarium would make an ideal home. It is more aquatic than most tree frogs, so you will have the fun of seeing your pet splashing in your small pond frequently.

Other Tree Frogs

There are many sorts of tree frogs and you can combine them in one tank or add one or two to tanks with more terrestrial or aquatic types, as their position up in the plant leaves will serve to avoid overcrowding and will balance the tank nicely. Some of the most interesting kinds are: the Cuban tree frog (*Hyla septentrionalis*), a large (5½″) species with a special fondness for humans; the European green tree frog (*Hyla arborea*), which changes color rapidly from a pale almost white or green and back again; the Mexican shovel-headed tree frog (*Diaglena reticulata*) with a skull that has an exaggerated bony thickening on top; the red-eyed tree frog (*Agalychnis callidryas*) of Mexico and Central America is brightly colored green with yellow bands on its sides and

The Mexican tree frog (*Smilisca baudini*).

145

orange legs edged at the top with a blue line — the eyes really are bright red; White's tree frog (*Hyla caerulea*) of Australia is less elaborately colored, being green with white dots on the back, but it is very shiny and is besides a gentle and loving pet; the marsupial frog (*Gastrotheca marsupiata*) of South America has a pouch on the back for the carrying of fertilized eggs; the Mexican tree frog (*Smilisca baudini*) has an amusing voice and frequently chuckles in its tank.

Tree frogs are usually quite happy in captivity and should be fed with small insects, appropriate to their own small size.

Cochranella
(Cochranella fleishmanni)

This interesting little frog with no common name comes from Central America. It has an almost transparent skin. You will be able to see the animal's heart beating. When you feed it, you will be able to watch the food moving through the digestive tract to the stomach.

Cochranella looks much like a tree frog and leads a similar existence, but along with several other related species it is placed in a separate family. It has adhesive pads on its toes and will cling to the undersides of a ready leaf in the terrarium.

The African Goliath Frog
(Cyclorana goliath)

This is the giant of all frogs. It is one of the Ranidae. Coming from the Belgian Congo, captive specimens measure ten inches and more. They live deep in the pools of the river and are not easy to nab. Besides, the natives value their thighbones as magical devices and are not eager to part with their catches. That probably accounts for their rarity and the accompanying high prices asked at pet stores.

The African goliath frog, like the American bullfrog, is a difficult pet to keep, for its large size and still larger appetite make feeding a problem.

The Spotted Hylambates
(*Hylambates maculatus*)

This hardy frog does very well in captivity. The bright red patches on its legs will add color to your bog terrarium. Find some moths to feed him occasionally and he will be very grateful.

In nature the spotted hylambates can be found in the southeastern part of Africa, from Mozambique to Zanzibar.

(*Phrynomerus bifasciatus*)

This interesting frog belongs to an African genus which includes several different species. *Phrynomerus bifasciatus* has unusual coloring. In bright light, the black is gray with a single dark stripe. Move it into a more shaded spot and it will develop orange and pink stripes on the gray base. Take it farther into the shade and there will be zebra stripes of black and red all over the body.

In nature, *Phrynomerus* hides in stumps or in termite nests, so be sure to put some sort of tunnel in your tank. For a real treat, feed your pet some houseflies. House it in a separate tank, for it has a skin secretion that is fatal to other frogs. It will also make your hands burn, so try to avoid handling.

This frog is unusual in its ability to move its neck and turn its head from side to side. It walks rather than hops, with its body high off the ground.

The Narrow-mouthed Toads
(Family Microhylidae)

There are many species in this family, well distributed about the globe. Because they have a great love of privacy, their habits are almost completely unknown. They will probably not make very endearing pets as they are extremely shy with humans. However, if you are an experienced amphibian-keeper and are interested in a serious study, raising a narrow-mouthed toad could be a most rewarding experience.

In the United States lives the eastern narrow-mouthed toad *(Gastrophryne carolinensis)* found from Maryland to Florida and west to Texas, and the Great Plains narrow-mouthed toad *(Gastrophryne olivacea)*. Other members of the group live in Mexico, South America, Asia and Africa, New Guinea and Madagascar.

Narrow-mouthed toads usually sleep in underground burrows during the day, so be sure to provide a hiding place in your terrarium. Some members of the group have long, pointed snouts and some do not, but all have the very narrow mouth that gives them their name. Those with the pointed noses use them for digging up ants, and *Gastrophryne olivacea* feeds almost exclusively on these small insects, so feeding should be no problem.

Common species or exotic, an amphibian makes a charming and rewarding pet. If you have to coax yours to eat at first, how pleased you will be later when he is eating from your hand. If your pet becomes ill and needs nursing, the bond between you will grow even stronger. The hours that you spend in the proximity of your terrarium can be among the most satisfying of your life.

Index

151

GEORG AND LISBETH ZAPPLER, authors of *The World After the Dinosaurs* and *Amphibians as Pets,* met while working at The American Museum of Natural History. Georg Zappler, a highly trained zoologist, has long been interested in communicating his ideas to the general public and, through the media of books, museum exhibits, and educational television, he has been able to realize his ambition. Lisbeth Zappler, who also wrote *The Natural History of the Tail,* began her career as a journalist at the age of sixteen and wanted to present complex scientific theories to children. The authors' mutual interest in animals is clearly demonstrated in the enormous number of pets to be found wandering inside and outside their New Jersey home. Their own children have been given a very intimate understanding of fish, frogs, lizards, birds, cats, dogs, and stray rabbits. It is in an endeavor to pass on some of this knowledge to other children that this book has been written.